Bob Sjogren and Gerald Robison have put together a parable, which is not only humorous, but profound. It helps redefine who we are in relationship to Christ in a way that is prophetic, yet easy to accept.

TONY CAMPOLO,
Professor Emeritus at Eastern University
and author of *It's Friday But Sunday's Comin'*

Cat and Dog Theology will help you reevaluate your relationship with the Master. This kind of obedience training is what the church needs, especially in 21st century America!

JOHN ANKERBURG,
Ankerburg Theological Institute

Many Christians today have lost sight of the fact that the ultimate purpose of man is to glorify God. In their marvelous book, Bob Sjogren and Gerald Robison show very clearly how our theology has deteriorated, and how we can be restored to a correct and dynamic belief and trust in our great God and Savior.

BILL BRIGHT,
Founder, Campus Crusade for Christ

Topics such as feel-good theology, suffering, fairness, "winner's-circle gospel," wrong priorities, and Christian humanism are dealt with in a fresh way that causes even the most seasoned theologian or missionary to ponder if he or she has not unwittingly been affected with this self-centered mindset. . . . At first the book's title made me skeptical about its contents. But once I began reading it, it was one book I could not put down. Its message is so important I now require all my missions students to read it, and recommend missionaries and mission committees to do so as well.

MARVIN J. NEWELL,
professor, Moody Graduate School,
as reviewed in EMQ Magazine

CAT & DOG THEOLOGY

THEOLOGY

Revised Edition

CAT & DOG THEOLOGY

Revised Edition

RETHINKING OUR RELATIONSHIP
WITH OUR MASTER

Bob Sjogren
and
Gerald Robison

IVP Books

An imprint of InterVarsity Press
Downers Grove, Illinois

InterVarsity Press
P.O. Box 1400, Downers Grove, IL 60515-1426
World Wide Web: www.ivpress.com
E-mail: email@ivpress.com

InterVarsity Press˚ is the book-publishing division of InterVarsity Christian Fellowship/USA˚, a movement of students and faculty active on campus at hundreds of universities, colleges and schools of nursing in the United States of America, and a member movement of the International Fellowship of Evangelical Students. For information about local and regional activities, write Public Relations Dept., InterVarsity Christian Fellowship/ USA, 6400 Schroeder Rd., P.O. Box 7895, Madison, WI 53707-7895, or visit the IVCF website at <www. intervarsity.org>.

Originally published in 2003 by Authentic Media.
Published in 2005 by Biblica.

ISBN 978-0-8308-5621-5

Printed in the United States of America ∞

Cataloging-in-Publication Data is available through the Library of Congress.

P	18	17	16	15	14	13	12	11	10	9	8	7	6	5	4	3
Y	27	26	25	24	23	22	21	20	19	18	17	16	15	14	13	

Author Dedications

This is dedicated to my wife, Sharon, who has been patient and forbearing with this ol' Dog. Throughout our time together, God has caused us to grow more like the godly Dogs this book speaks of, and we've been "kennel mates" for thirty-three years now. She has served as my friend, mate, navigator, inspiration, provider of sermon illustrations, the mother of my children, and the keeper of my home and heart. I look forward to growing old with her (even though I'll get there more quickly) and to helping her become all God wants her to be as she does the same for me.

Gerald

I'd like to dedicate this book to my bride of over twenty years and to my four wonderful, fantastic kids!

Debby, you've been such a faithful friend, sticking with me in the good times and the bad times. You have lived out Dog Theology to me in such a real, tangible way. Thanks for being such a wonderful friend, such a terrific mother, and such a godly person. I'm so glad you said, "I do," so many years ago. No husband could ever ask for more.

And to Luke, Elise, Abby, and Hunter, you are each so wonderful, and I love you so dearly. Thanks for putting up with all of the "recording sessions" I made you go through(!), thanks for all the laughter in our home, and thanks for helping us build such wonderful family memories. I know God is pleased.

Bob/Dad

Contents

The Eleven Dangers of Cat Theology
—Where Things Go Wrong!

When Cat Theology Goes From "Incomplete" to "Incorrect"

A New Twist
—Individually and Corporately Glorifying God

Preface

As you read this book, keep in mind that the information in this book is also available through our live seminars, which are held in many countries around the world. UnveilinGLORY, a ministry of ACMC (Advancing Churches in Mission Commitment), has men and women trained and ready to visit churches to teach on Cat and Dog Theology. Consider having them come to your church. It would be a great way to help your church to stop thinking like Cats and start living like Dogs for the glory of God! For more information, please visit our web site at www.CatandDogTheology. com.

Introduction

The theme of this book is based on the notable differences between what may be two of mankind's (if not God's) favorite creatures: cats and dogs.

Knowing that there are animal lovers of each, we hope that no one takes offense at our acknowledging the different traits of these beloved creatures, for certainly no offense is intended. Rather, we merely recognize that the God-given traits of cats and dogs can be similar to certain theological attitudes held by many Christians.

In nature, these attitudes are suitable to both felines and canines. But in our theology, some attitudes may draw us closer to God, and others actually pull us *away* from Him.

We hope you learn to differentiate these attitudes, and, as a result, draw closer to the God who delights in you (as well as to cats and dogs!).

1

Cat and Dog Theology

When Debby and I (Bob) lived in Phoenix, Arizona, mowing our front yard took no longer than ten minutes from start to finish, and that included raking the grass! Because our postage-stamp lawn was so small, we never got a dog. But when we found out we would be moving to Richmond, Virginia, we promised our four kids that we would get both a dog and a cat. And we made good on that promise!

We love our dog and cat.

Jasmine is a white mixed Labrador. We rescued her from the pound, and she has become a part of our family. She loves to run in the lawn and is the official welcoming committee greeting us when we drive up in the car.

After we had Jasmine, we were on the way to piano practice one day when we saw a sign for kittens. Well, we now have a cat. Simba too has won his way into our hearts. Simba loves to sleep on the kitchen chairs and can be found on our beds at night.

But I've noticed that dogs and cats are very different.

Any time I turn into my drive way, my dog Jasmine jumps out of her dog house and runs to the car parading around as the official welcoming committee. She'll run parallel to the car until it comes to a stop. Then she barks until I open the door. Once open, she puts her front paws into the car where I begin to scratch her behind the ears. As I do this, her tail begins to wag feverishly. We enjoy the brief moments together, and it's evident to anyone watching that we share a deep bond and love!

When I go into my house and walk into the same room where our cat is, there's no evidence of love from the cat toward me. I'll make a loud kissing noise toward the cat, but the cat won't even acknowledge me. In fact, he doesn't even move. Any acknowledgment that he does give me comes in the form of walking over toward me and "marking" my leg with his head which is his way of saying, "I own you, pal." But then he'll then go and "mark" a chair. (It's rather humbling to be relegated to the importance of a chair in my cat's life, all I am to my cat is warm-blooded furniture!) Yes, they're quite different.

There is a big distinction in the way they go outside as well.

When Jazzy wants to go outside, she jumps at the kitchen door and barks, letting you know she wants outside. When the door is opened, she bolts out the door and runs into the yard.

When Simba wants out, he stands by the window next to the front door. That is the signal that it is time to let the cat out. So I go to the front door, open it, and proceed to open the second screen door. What does Simba do? Nothing. He just sits there and looks outside (knowing full well I've opened the door). After staring outside for a while, he'll look inside for a while as if saying, "Am I sure I really want to go outside?" He'll then look back outside and occasionally lick his paw. (I think he's checking some kind of cat watch—I'm not sure.)

Now, patience isn't one of my greatest strengths, so I call out his name, make some kissing noises, and wait some more. Again, Simba looks outside through the window and then looks at the open door, then back outside, and then inside. He will repeat this process a few times. Finally, with no sense of urgency, he will cautiously walk over to the inner door and slowly make his way to the beginning of the great outdoors. And in the process, he'll take great patience to mark the door.

Yet right before he takes the final steps to his new destination, he stops and sits. He'll then look outside, then inside, then outside, then inside, and then back up at me. This too can be repeated a couple of times. All the while I am holding the door open and waiting. (Now remember, patience isn't one of my greatest strengths.) I finally get so frustrated that I end up kicking the cat out the door (lovingly, of course, because my kids may be watching me!).

What I've heard others say, I claim is true: dogs have masters, but cats have staff. This is why mankind has traditionally attributed characteristics such as loyalty, service, and faithfulness to dogs. But cats have acquired traits like independence and aloofness. There's a joke about cats and dogs that conveys their differences perfectly. A dog says, "You pet me, you feed me, you shelter me, you love me, you must be God." A cat says, "You pet me, you feed me, you shelter me, you love me, I must be God."

This difference between cats and dogs is very similar to how Christian theology is being lived out today. We call it "Dog Theology" and "Cat Theology." Dogs say, "Lord, You love me, You bless me abundantly, You gave Your life for me, You must be God." Whereas Cats say, "Lord, You love me, You bless me abundantly, You gave your life for me, I must be god."

Did you notice the little "g" in god? Please note that Cats, or people with this theology, never really say, "I must be God." They know it would be politically and biblically incorrect. That's why pure Cat Theology is never taught from the pulpit. It is never sung in a song. It is never taught as a seminar. This is because while Cats never say, "I must be God," they do say, "It's all about me" or "It's all about us! God did all this for us!

Life is about us! I must be what God not only died for but lives for too!"

Obedience, Glory, and Blessings

Now, in order to understand how Dog and Cat Theologies differ, you need to understand that both Cats and Dogs want obedience in their lives but in different ways. Dogs learn to obey their masters. Cats want their masters to obey them. As the joke goes, dogs have masters, but cats have staff. Theologically, Dogs want to obey God, but Cats want God to obey them.

DeVern Fromke, in his excellent book *Unto Full Stature,* says it this way: "Today we are reaping a harvest of man-centered conversions because we are more concerned for man than for God. . . . We are more interested in God serving man than man serving God."[1] You can see this attitude reflected in Cats' prayer lives. The focus is on their lives, their needs, and their wants. Their prayers contain lots of *me's* and *my's*. (We'll address this more in later chapters.)

In *Praying Like Jesus*, James Mulholland writes, "In December, I addressed my requests to Santa Claus; the rest of the year I petitioned God. My real concern is how to get God to give me what I want. My desire is to manipulate God rather than to know him. . . . Prayer is about me: Bless me. Protect me. Take care of me."[2] Martin Luther, a man used by God to spark the greatest reformation in the history of Christianity, said, "The essence of sin is that man seeks his own in everything, even in God."

Yes, Cats are in it for themselves. And they would never say it, but if someone or something could give them a better life than following Christ, they would seriously consider it. Why? For Cats, life is primarily not about God, it is about them. Cats are into Christianity far more for what they can get out of it than for the opportunity to radiate the glory of the King of Heaven.

Dogs say, "No, it's about God's glory," and they learn from Paul in Romans. In Romans 15:8–9, Paul speaks about Christ's death. He says: "For I tell you that Christ has become a servant of the Jews on behalf of God's truth, to confirm the promises made to the patriarchs so that . . ."

Stop right there. Note what is happening here. He is proclaiming the reason *why* Christ came to the earth: to live a perfect life and die a painful death. This is an important key. What is the reason? He says, "so that the Gentiles" (odds are that this pertains to the majority of those reading this book) *"might not go to hell."*

Wrong. That's not what the text says, but what a perfect place for Paul to have said it! If that's not what Paul said, then what *did* he say? He said, "so that the Gentiles *may glorify God for his mercy"* (emphasis added). All of us are saved for a reason: so that we might glorify God for His mercy. There is a purpose to our salvation, and that purpose is not just about escaping hell.

If It Were about Us . . .

Cats are missing the forest because they are so focused on the trees. They are so focused on the day-to-day glimpses of creation that they are missing the big picture. Think about it. If you were God and you were going to create an environment for humanity, wouldn't you design everything for them? But when we look around, we see that it's not designed for us; it's designed for God. "For by him all things were created: things in heaven and on earth, visible and invisible, whether thrones or powers or rulers or authorities; all things were created by him and *for* him" (Colossians 1:16, emphasis added). He shares it with us, but it's for Him!

If it were about us, why did God create three-quarters of the earth to be covered with water? Think about it. We humans can't even exist on three-quarters of the earth's surface. Think about it. If God made this world for us, wasn't it rather dumb to make it in such a way that we can't even exist on three-quarters of the earth? God wasn't dumb. It's not for us, it's for Him!

And what about everything in the water? That's for Him too! That's why when you pull a sword fish out of the water, its colors are bright and brilliant and beautiful, but they only last 30 seconds because the sun fades them out. The beauty of a sword fish was designed to be seen by God in the water, not by us! Its beauty is for God.

If it were about us, why are there sounds our ears can't hear while Dogs can hear them. If this life and creation were all about us, why would God have done that? Why did God create the eagle to have better eyesight than we? That doesn't seem fair. Why can a baby horse walk at birth, but we humans take nine months just to learn how to crawl? Didn't God know we had places to go, people to see, and things to do? (I'm still trying to catch up!)

Why do our bodies wear out? Why did God design us to be completely dependent on others when we start out, to reach our prime somewhere in the middle years, and then to have our bodies and minds wear out as our older years greet us? Why did God create us to need sleep? Did you know that a giraffe sleeps for only five minutes at a time, totaling less than two hours a day? God could have created us like that, but He didn't. He chose to have us spend eight hours a day horizontal, conked out, and oblivious to the rest of the world. What a waste of time for those of us "doers."

Why are there galaxies we can't even see? Come on, God, that wasn't too smart if it were all about us! And why can't we change our appearance like the chameleon? Why can't we say, "I want to look African. I want to look Asian. I want to look Caucasian. I want to look Latino," or "Lord, I just want more hair."

God created it just the way He likes it because it's not about us! It's about Him, and He does it all because it pleases Him! "You are worthy, our Lord and God, to receive glory and honor and power, for you created all things, and *for your pleasure* they were created and have their being" (Revelation 4:11, our translation).

Glimpses in Revelation

In John's glimpse of heaven in Revelation 4, we learn some very humbling yet challenging and freeing things. John is seeing the four living creatures giving glory to God in verse 8. They cry out, "Holy, holy, holy is the Lord God Almighty, who was, and is, and is to come" (Revelation 4:8). No reference to us humans? None at all.

Why didn't those living creatures of Revelation mention us? The answer is simple: they are so caught up in the glory and wonder of God that nothing else matters! It is all about God and His wonderful majesty! (Why would they even care if we exist?) When the elders see this happening, they join in. Notice what they say.

> Whenever the living creatures give glory and honor and thanks to Him who sits on the throne, who lives forever and ever, the twenty-four elders fall down before Him who sits on the throne and worship Him who lives forever and ever, and cast their crowns before the throne, saying: "You are worthy, O Lord, To receive glory and honor and power; For You created all things, And by Your will they exist and were created." (Revelation 4:9–11 NKJV)

That phrase "by Your will they exist and were created" could just as easily be translated as "for your pleasure they were created and have their being."

Everything that God created, He created for His pleasure! You know what that means? It means the following:

- Dogs hear sounds our ears can't hear because it pleases Him.
- The majority of the earth is covered with water because it brings pleasure to the Creator.
- Eagles have better eyesight than humans because it puts a smile on God's face.
- The baby horse walks at birth while baby humans can't even crawl for nine months because God wants it that way.
- Our bodies wear out because it forces us to put our hope in God, the only One who is worthy of glory.
- We sleep to remind us that we are not God, who neither slumbers nor sleeps.
- The galaxies exist in awesome splendor to bring pleasure to the One who created them all and has each star named.
- We can't change our appearance because if we could, we would be so caught up in ourselves, we would totally forget about the One who is worthy of glory, honor, and praise.

Life is not about us. It is about God!

2

Some Differences between Cat and Dog Theology

Many years ago, I pastored a church in Australia. Sharon and I had been there long enough for the people to know certain things about us. Two things stuck out about me to one particular couple. They knew I hated certain vegetables, and they knew that I had a sense of humor. They learned that I could not only dish out humor liberally, but I could also receive it freely!

One evening we were having dinner with this couple from our church. The wife had labored hard preparing one of my favorite Australian desserts, Pavlova. Now for those of you who aren't familiar with this wonderful delicacy, Pavlova is like a cake, but it has a hard meringue on the outside.

After wonderful fellowship with dinner, our hostess brought out coffee and dessert. When I saw it, my eyes lit up. Pavlova! I couldn't wait to take my first bite. While I was engaged in conversation with her husband, she cut me a piece and placed it on my plate.

When my fork went into the cake, I noticed some small, hard pieces of something but was too engaged to pay any attention to them. I noticed that this couple was looking at me, but I was too engrossed to pay attention to that either. But after putting it in my mouth, I quickly realized why they were both staring at me! Our hostess had put cauliflower inside the middle of the white cake! That Pavlova is a perfect parallel to Cats and Dogs in the church today. It is very difficult to tell the difference between a Cat and a Dog on the outside. Why? On the outside, Cats and Dogs look just alike—you can't tell by looking which is which. They both have invited Christ into their lives. They both go to church. They both pray. They both have quiet times. They both do everything pretty much the same on the outside. But on the inside, there is an entirely different attitude. One says, "It's all about me," and the other says, "It's all about God."

Two Ways to Heaven

In our churches, one difference between people with Cat Theology and people with Dog Theology is clearly seen in what moves them toward heaven. Dogs and Cats get to heaven with very different motivations. Although there is only one way to heaven, there can be different reasons for wanting to get there.

Cats see the option of hell and walk, or run, away from it. If hell is on the far right and heaven is on the far left, Cats are moving from the right to the left (going toward heaven); but, they are walking backwards, focused on hell. A Cat says, "I don't want to go to hell. I don't want to go to hell. I don't want to go to hell."

Cats find out they can invite Christ into their lives, so they bow their heads and say a prayer. Then they slap some faith onto it and say, "Praise the Lord, we're not going to hell." When Cats do this, they are primarily focused on themselves. Their focus is only on their lives. They only catch glimpses of Christ as they glance over their shoulders. Although it's not a bad start, it falls far short of what God wants.

You see, Dogs want to get to heaven for a different reason.

Dogs are also moving away from hell toward heaven, going from the right to the left, but they walk forward. Hell is behind them. Heaven is in front of them. A Dog says, "I've found Someone who's not only beautiful, He is beauty. I've found Someone not only powerful, He's almighty. I've found Someone who not only loves, He is love. I've got to give my life to Him."

A Dog's salvation is described in Matthew 13:44: "The kingdom of heaven is like treasure hidden in a field. When a man found it, he hid it again, and then *in his joy went and sold all he had and bought that field*" (emphasis added).

Notice that the man first found the treasure, and *then* he went and sold all he had and bought the field. He did all this out of joy. In his *joy* he sold all he had and bought the field. Why? He had found a treasure that was of greater worth than all the other things he possessed. He joyfully relinquished all other possessions to obtain this one great treasure.

When we give seminars, we always ask the question, "How many of you know Christians who are totally joyless?" The majority of people in our audiences raise their hands. We have discovered one reason why so many Christians are joyless. Their salvation is basically fire insurance, and they are merely walking away from hell, focused on themselves. They have never discovered the treasure. Think about it. There is no joy in walking away from hell. Relief? Yes. Joy? No.

Assurance of Salvation

The very assurance of salvation differs between a Cat and a Dog. Many Cats know they are Christians because they "prayed the prayer." A conversation with them could go something like this:

"So you are a Christian, right?"

"Oh yes," says the Cat. "I prayed the prayer. I remember I was in sixth grade. The pastor gave the invitation, and something made me move out of my seat. I knew it was God. Tears were rolling down my face. I walked up to the front and gave my life to Jesus."

"How's your life now?"

"Oh, not too good," says the Cat with a hesitant, hurting voice. "I'm going through a divorce. The kids are taking the brunt of it. I don't want to hurt them, but I just can't live with that person."

"Well, how are your quiet times?"

"Umm, I'm not having any. I know I should be, but, quite honestly, I'm angry with God, even bitter toward Him."

"But you're a Christian?"

"Oh yes, I prayed the prayer."

This salvation works its way out to the point that when someone asks a Cat, "Are you a Christian?" they say, "Yeah, I'm saved!" What are Cats communicating? Christianity is all about being saved from hell. Christianity's focus is to keep them from going to hell, and everything still revolves around their lives.

Dogs respond very differently when asked if they're Christians. A conversation with a Dog might go something like this:

"Are you a Christian?"

"Oh yes," says the Dog.

"How do you know?"

"Oh, I'm passionate for Christ, and I want nothing more than to see His glory shine. I want to see it shine in the work place. I want to see it radiate at home, through my family, in every area of my life, and I want to see it go to all the nations of the earth."

"Did you pray a prayer?"

"When I was a little kid, I did. But it wasn't until I got to college that I found God to be so wonderful and so amazing that I would willingly and joyfully give up anything and everything to please Him!"

Cats prove their salvation with a prayer they prayed and trust in that to prove they are believers, which they may very well be. Dogs demonstrate their salvation by the facts that they hunger for God, want more and more of Him in their lives, and want Him to shine through their lives. These desires guarantee that they are believers.

Prayer

Cats and Dogs see prayer quite differently too. In fact, Dogs and Cats can pray the exact same prayers but have two distinct meanings. Take, for example, the prayer, "Dear Lord, we just ask You to bless our church."

Immediately there should be warning flags. Cats are only praying for *their* church and not for the greater kingdom of God, for other churches in their area, or for the world. In many churches, the focus is always (and only) on *their* church. But aside from this, their prayers can be different. Remember outwardly it is difficult to tell who is a Dog and who is a Cat in the church. It is only inwardly that we can see the differences.

Inwardly, this is what a Cat could be praying: "Father, You know we need a new gymnasium for the youth; and, God, our parking is so crammed, we're losing people (our numbers are going down); and, God, the organ is really getting old (not to mention the carpeting). We just ask You to put it on the hearts of some rich people in our church to give until it hurts so that we'll receive Your blessings."

But God could be hearing something far different in the same prayer from a Dog. When a Dog says, "Dear Lord, we just ask You to bless our church," he could mean something like this: "Lord, give us wisdom in reaching the young people in our area, and give our youth a hunger and vision for taking Your glory overseas; and, Lord, show us which people group You'd like us to adopt; Father, we also pray for a foothold into the inner city—we see so little glory shining in that area; and there are so many international families living here, show us how to reach them for Your glory."

Cats are basically saying, "Dear Lord, we come boldly before You and ask You to help us build our kingdom." Cats pray for the things they desire, the things that will make life more comfortable and easy. It sounds like, "Father, please give me . . . , please let me . . . , please bring me . . . ."

15

Dogs boldly come before God as well, but they say, "Lord, we're here with great faith because we need things from You to help advance Your kingdom. We want to make You famous. We know You will answer our prayers."

It sounds like, "Father, let Your glory shine in this sickness. Allow Your glory to shine in how I'm treating my parents, my spouse, my kids. Father, Your glory is not shining in South Africa, in all of North Africa, in India, or in Pakistan; so, Father, raise up laborers to take Your glory to the ends of the earth."

John Piper has referred to the prayer life of many people (Cats) as a domestic intercom, by which a family can ask for requests from the kitchen. Prayer is much more than asking God to bring us goodies from the kitchen. Yet this is how many Cats use it. Dogs use prayer for God's sake to advance His kingdom, not theirs.

One church in Colorado lived out Cat Theology by taking money out of the missions fund (God's kingdom), causing missionaries to not get their support, and putting it toward a new organ (their kingdom). They had prayed so hard for a new organ that they rationalized away the need for missions and focused on themselves. (This church closed its doors a few years later.)

Do Dogs ever pray for blessings? Yes, but it is not their primary focus; it is a secondary focus. And when they pray for themselves, it is usually so that they can have a greater impact in the lives of others. Do Dogs ever pray for nicer cars and bigger homes? Yes, but only when there is a real need for them, not when there is merely a desire for them.

Worship

Worship too is quite different for Cats and Dogs. In Cat Theology, Cats worship Him for what He's done for them. It sounds like this: "Thank You for all the great things You've done for me. You have provided for me; You have protected me; You have given me this and that and more. Thanks!" Now there's nothing wrong with that unless that's all you are thinking about. It's all about you, you, you.

But in Dog Theology, Dogs worship God primarily for who He is and secondarily for what He has done for them. It sounds like this: "Oh Father, You are an amazing God. You are both merciful and just. Your creativity is awesome and Your splendor is magnificent. And Father, You are a God of love. You love the Muslims, the Hindus, the Buddhists, and You love us! We honor You and all that You stand for. May all people worship You for who You are!"

You'll be amazed at how many songs you'll now recognize that were written with a Cat-Theology perspective. So many worship songs contain the themes of *I*, *me*, and *my*. These songs have words that focus primarily on what the worshiper is getting from the Lord.

Are these songs wrong? Not necessarily. It depends on the worshiper's perspective. A Cat and Dog can sing the very same song but with totally different perspectives. A Cat focuses on personal glory while a Dog focuses on God's glory.

One pastor heard the "Cat and Dog Theology" message on a Sunday morning. On Monday morning, he went into his office to get some work done and turned on his music. After five minutes, he was so disgusted with the particular CD he was listening to—it was full of a Cat's perspective—that he turned it off. (We apologize if this is ruining your music selection!) Understanding Dog Theology can cause you to rethink your perspective about everything in your life!

Lordship

Let's look at another difference between Cat and Dog Theology: Lordship. In Cat Theology, God's Lordship is very limited. You see, Cats love to serve God when it is fun. They know it is good for their souls and that God is pleased with it. But when it quits being fun, they quit calling Him "Lord" and don't serve Him as they should. He is Lord as long as they are being blessed.

Don't miss the fact that Cats want to be close to God. They want Lordship, but they don't want it to interfere with their lives. When it starts to interfere, He's no longer Lord. Oh, Cats will keep playing the Christian game. They'll keep going to church; they'll still say, "Praise the Lord"; but in their hearts, they'll do what makes life comfortable for them.

But in Dog Theology, He has complete Lordship—anytime, anywhere, anyplace. Dogs obey even when they don't want to, even if it means going overseas. Dogs are very aware that when they found the treasure, its value meant more to them than life or the things in life! And when Dogs are asked to jump, they only ask how high. They obey wholeheartedly. Why? They have found a treasure in God, and their focus is on pleasing Him.

Half of God

Here's another difference between Cats and Dogs: Cats only know "half of God." What does this mean? They focus on God's love, mercy, and grace but never on His hatred of sin, wrath, and judgment. A Cat doesn't want to acknowledge, and therefore doesn't focus on, any aspect of God that would make life uncomfortable. Just take one of these unwanted aspects as an example, like God's judgment of sin.

Cats would never think of God judging them. "God wouldn't judge me. He loves me! He died for me! He won't judge me." Cats in America cannot comprehend the thought that God would judge America in their lifetimes. (They'd never say it, but they almost think God is an American Himself!) They are so focused on God's love that they have never taken time to realize that God hates their sin.

As a nation, America is stuck in Cat Theology. If you really stop and think about it, America is basically communicating to God the following messages:

- Lord, we don't want You in our government; we've separated the church from the state.
- Lord, we don't want You in our schools; sorry, no children can pray there.
- Lord, we don't want You in our wombs; Your definition of life and ours is very different, and anyway, a woman has to have the right of free choice.
- And, Lord, we are going to print pornography and send it all over the world, along with our television shows that promote lifestyles contrary to Your Word, because, Lord, we have freedom of speech.
- But, dear Lord, the terrorists are attacking; please bless us and protect us.

How hypocritical! Singing "God Bless America" is a contradiction when we have kicked Him out of our government, schools, and wombs, when we are the number one exporter of pornography, and when we have produced television shows that reek with lifestyles the Lord abhors. You see, Cats want the perks (God's blessings and protection) but none of the responsibilities (God's laws). It is all about them!

Dogs are very conscious of the fact that God judges. They saw Him judge David when he counted his fighting men, and seventy thousand other men died as a result (1 Chronicles 21:1–17). They know God judged Moses for striking the rock when he was supposed to merely speak to it (Numbers 20:9–12).

Dogs are aware that His Holiness will not put up with disobedience in those He loves, and, yes, He judges those He loves as well. Dogs see the terrorists' attack as a loving God sending a wake-up call to America, judging a very few (3 thousand in the 9/11 attack) so that the rest of America (290 million) would repent. Maybe now is the time to change our call from "God, bless America" to "America, bless God!"

Would You Like More Differences?

For Cats, success is defined by human standards. How big is our church? How many baptisms are we having each year? How many come to our Sunday schools? Dogs define success by divine standards. The question is not, How big is our church? but, Are the people we shepherd obeying the Lord and worshiping Him?

For Cats, repentance is out, and self-esteem is in. For Dogs, repentance is a part of life, and holiness is in.

Cats hunger to be entertained in the church. Dogs hunger to worship God and reflect His glory.

Cats love head knowledge. Bible trivia is fun. They can quote multiple facts found in the Bible, but they are lacking in the area of application. Dogs love that which draws them closer to God. They are more interested in obeying the Lord than simply knowing about Him.

Cats want the full picture before they obey God. Dogs are happy to obey the little the Lord gives.

Cats believe the Church is at peace. Dogs believe the Church is at war.

Cats believe in arbitrary truth—it changes as the wind changes. Dogs believe in absolute truth—it never changes for them.

Cats have a "feel-good" theology. Dogs have an "obedience" theology.

Cats deter their kids from the mission field. Dogs encourage them into the mission field.

Cats can't envision a loving God sending anyone to hell. Dogs know that hell exists because God is holy, just, and promises to judge sin.

Some Cats can't imagine why God would cause anyone to suffer eternally for a finite set of sins. Dogs know that hell is eternal because an infinite glory has been rejected.

Cats see an immigrant family moving in next door and think, "There goes the neighborhood." Dogs see it as an opportunity to reveal God's glory to people from another culture.

Cats want their children to bring them glory. Dogs want their children to bring God glory.

Cats see a job as a means of attaining wealth. Dogs see a job as a ministry opportunity.

Cats think God is a means to an end. Dogs think God is the end.

These differences could go on and on.

Warning

So are you a Cat or are you a dog? Odds are, you aren't either, you are somewhere in between.

Over the years, we've seen this material get 'abused' by causing an "us/them" mentality. Instead of using this to encourage us all to become more like God and live for His glory, some have used it to judge others by calling them "cats" with the implied assumption, "I'm a perfect dog."

As Jim Thurber (our International Director of UnveilinGLORY) says in his version of the live seminar, "We're all cats having moments of 'dog-dom'!" Or another way of saying it is that some people are cats with moments of "dog-dom", some people are dogs who slip back into their "cat-ish" ways! We are all somewhere in between. One sweet elderly lady claimed she wasn't a cat or a dog, but thought of herself as a puppy. It was her attempt to address what we are saying here.

Never let this be used to create an "us/them" mentality and divide the body of Christ. Remember, there's cat in all of us to varying degrees. Let us all walk in humility and see it more as an "us/us" situation and encourage others, and ourselves, to become more like Christ!

3

Not Incorrect, Just Incomplete

Sharon and I (Gerald) have an unusual sense of humor that has run rampant through our marriage and its years of precious memories. We are often telling jokes and pulling pranks. (Okay, I tell the jokes and pull the pranks, but she listens and joyfully bears the brunt of the punch line or practical joke.)

Our sleeping habits vary. She's a morning person, and I'm a night person. I scoot into the bed long after she's asleep and tumble out long after she's awake. But I do try to turn down the bed for her before she gets there, and I try to make the bed when I get up.

One day she must have recognized my sneaky smile and asked what I was up to. I just continued smiling and tried not to give anything away. She prodded me more about what I had done and what I was thinking. But, again, I just smiled. She kept after me until I broke down and told her, "Oh, nothing. I just made the bed for you." But I guess my snicker kept her suspicions up.

"What have you done?" she asked.

"Nothing. Just made the bed!" I answered.

"Did you short-sheet the bed again?"

"No."

"Well, what did you do?"

"Nothing. I just made the bed."

"Did you steal my pillow?"

"No."

"Did you steal the covers?"

"No."

"What *did* you do?"

"Nothing. You're so suspicious." More snickering and a mischievous smile continue to ease out of me.

"I'm going to see."

Upstairs she went, and that's when the laughter poured out of the bedroom. You see I made the bed, but only the half I slept on. There it was: straight, neat, and nearly perfect on one side and crumpled, tossed, and full of wrinkles on the other.

My statement, "I made the bed," was not incorrect, but it was incomplete. It only gave a part of the whole picture, which was a distortion of the way it really was.

On a lot of courtroom television dramas when a person is sworn in, they are asked to "tell the truth, the whole truth, and nothing but the truth." This—the whole truth—provides an accurate picture of something. Cat Theology doesn't provide an accurate, whole picture of God's Word, His will, or His ways. Cat Theology is not incorrect, but it is incomplete. And in being incomplete, it is a distortion of what He wants and what He has to say to us. Let's see how this works in the Christian life.

Cats are saved from hell, but their version of the gospel stops there. Once they're saved, they think "Hallelujah! Praise God, I'm going to heaven." But for Dogs, getting saved is merely a stepping stone to what the true purpose of life and the gospel is all about. Dogs are saved from hell for worshiping God and glorifying Him. They know that their salvation has a single purpose: to glorify

God by enjoying His presence and worshiping Him. And Dogs learn to do that twenty-four hours a day, seven days a week.

Now there is a huge difference between being saved *from* something and being saved *for* something. When you are saved *from* something, the focus is on you, what *you* get out of it. Salvation is all about the following:

- you not going to hell
- you not having to pay the penalty you deserve
- you getting God's mercy
- you receiving God's grace
- you getting to be with God for all eternity
- you having Christ prepare a place for you in His Father's mansion

When you are saved for something, you know and agree with all of the above, but your focus is on God. With a God-centered focus, your salvation goes a step further:

- pointing to God's mercy
- worshiping Him
- giving Him the glory He deserves
- lifting His name on high
- exalting Him for His greatness
- singing His praise for ever and ever

Now is there anything wrong with being saved *from* hell? No, but it can't stop there. By itself, it is incomplete. Cat Theology is only about us getting to heaven. Dog Theology includes that but also goes beyond it to radiating and revealing the glory of God.

Prayers

Incomplete Cat Theology can come out in our prayers. Listen to this prayer: "Dear Lord, thank You for dying on the cross for our sins. Amen." Did you notice the period after "sins"? That period stands for "complete; end of thought; it's done." There is no indication as to *why* He died on the cross for our sins, and therefore it implies that it is about us. That prayer is not incorrect, but it is incomplete.

When Dogs hear that prayer, they want to cry out, "Finish the prayer! Finish the prayer! He died on the cross for our sins *so that* we might honor Him, we might glorify Him, and so that we might point to Him for His mercy!" But Cats are only worried about their sins, so they finish the prayer being thankful their sins have been forgiven and miss the bigger reason of why Christ died for them: "So that the Gentiles may glorify God for his mercy" (Romans 15:9).

Blessings

Cat Theology has an incomplete view of blessings. God blesses us for a reason. Genesis 12 reveals why God blessed Abraham (Abram).

> I will make you into a great nation
>> and I will bless you;
> I will make your name great,
>> and *you will be a blessing.*
> I will bless those who bless you,
>> and whoever curses you I will curse;
> and *all peoples on earth*
>> *will be blessed through you.* (Genesis 12:2–3,
> emphasis added)

God blessed Abraham *so that* he would be a blessing, not just to those around him but to all the peoples of the earth. God blesses us for that same reason. We are blessed to be a blessing. God wants that blessing to pass through us to the very ends of the earth.

Cats want to gather the blessings in a bucket and keep them for themselves. But blessings were never designed to be hoarded in a bucket. Dogs see themselves as a garden hose, or pipeline, whose purpose is to be filled with water and to carry it elsewhere, not as the faucet that only opens and dispenses blessings for itself. Dogs enjoy the blessings and pass them on to others.

Dogs see themselves as a conduit, or pipeline, of blessings. They understand that God has a plan for the blessings He presents to us. God knows whom He wants to bless *through* you tomorrow, next week, next year, and for the rest of your life! He sees through you to others and wants others to see Him through you. He desires to be made known to people of every tongue, every tribe, and every nation. This is one of the key reasons God wants to bless you.

But Cats stop short of the greater goal to be a blessing to others, and that leaves God's goal incomplete. They like to keep the blessings for themselves instead of passing them on. You can see this incompleteness all throughout the Sunday school lessons we are taught from the Scriptures. Take, for example, Daniel in the lions' den. What lesson do we learn from it? God will take care of us in times of trouble. This lesson is not incorrect, but it is incomplete. Why? It only focuses on what God is doing for us—His desire to bless us. What has been left out is the reason why God blesses us!

You remember the story. The king finds out who the bad guys are, and he takes Daniel out of the lions' den and throws the bad guys in. He then writes a memo from his desk and sends it to all of the kings of the earth saying, "I issue a decree that in every part of my kingdom people must fear and reverence the God of Daniel" (Daniel 6:26). What's happening here? You've got a Gentile king who is making God famous to all of the other Gentile kings around the world.

This is the other lesson we can learn from Daniel and the lions' den: as God takes care of you, people from different countries and cultures will be so impressed that they will go and tell others in their country about your God! How do Dogs apply it to their lives? They teach that we should get to know the people from other countries and cultures living around us and let them see our lives so that we can make God famous to them. But Cats rarely learn that lesson. They seem quite content to "be blessed." What they have learned is not incorrect, but it is incomplete.

Do you need another example? How about when Solomon asks God for wisdom instead of carnal pleasures and gets blessings in addition to the wisdom? What do Cats learn from this? As they seek wisdom from God, He is going to bless them in addition to the wisdom. While this is true, it's only half of the story. What's the other half?

Dogs find it linked to Solomon's reputation. Solomon was greater in riches and wisdom than all the other kings on the face of the earth. As a result, others came from the farthest regions to see the wisdom God had given to him (1 Kings 10:23–24). Solomon basically held "international wisdom seminars." (Don Richardson, the missionary, author, and speaker, coined that phrase.) What does Proverbs tell us about what Solomon taught? "The *fear* of the LORD is the beginning of *wisdom*, and knowledge of the Holy One is understanding" (Proverbs 9:10). Solomon made God famous and blessed the other nations with the knowledge of God.

How can this apply to us? God has blessed America with some of the greatest insights and technologies so that people from all over the world come to our backyard to study. And yet while this is a great opportunity to make God famous to the international students living among us, International Students Incorporated is telling us that 70 to 80 percent of all international students are never invited into an American home. Why? We are steeped in Cat Theology. Cats are so focused on how they can be blessed by God that they never have time to think of people from other countries, much less to invite them to become a part of their lives and from that to make God famous!

Do you need even more examples? How about being still before God (Psalm 46:10)? You know it; fill in the rest of the verse. "Be still, and _____ ; _____ _____. Odds are you didn't fill in the rest of the verse. Oh sure, you got the "know that I am God" part, but that's only the first third of the verse. What does the rest of it say? "Be still, and know that I am God; I will be exalted among the nations, I will be exalted in the earth." That's the rest of Psalm 46:10, but few people know it.

Why? Cat Theology has kept us focused only on what God does for us and not on what God wants to do in and through us. What does the verse mean? It means that as you are still before the Lord, as you are having quiet times alone with Him, as you are worshiping Him for His glory, He wants you to focus on seeing His glory go to all the nations of the earth, for He declares that it will!

You are to be praying that His glory will shine in the 10/40 Window. You are to be concerned about what is happening in all of the world. You are to be lifting up the needs of the Hindu world, the Buddhist world, the Chinese world, and all the other areas untouched with the gospel. You are to be asking God for laborers because the harvest is plentiful, but the laborers are few. What Cats have learned is not incorrect, but it is incomplete. There is another half of the gospel for Cats to learn!

There are many more stories in the Bible, but many Christians have only learned half of what there is to learn. As far as lessons go, Cats have another half of the Bible to discover! To learn more about this, please read *Unveiled At Last* by Bob Sjogren and get a much better understanding of that missing half.[3]

Incorrect Examples and Teaching

Where do we learn much of this incorrect teaching and theology? We learn it from the examples around us. It usually comes not from what is said but from what is *not* said.

At a large Christian conference of twenty thousand young people in the early nineties, a telephone call was made to another Christian conference of a similar size. The audience was waiting as the speaker kept saying, "Hello. Hello, are you there?" Finally the connection was made. "Yes, we're here." And then the very first words were spoken from the speaker in the United States.

"How is God blessing?" The response heard was all about God's blessings to them as a group. All good, all healthy, but something was missing. The question was not incorrect, but it was incomplete. Not once did the speaker say, "How is God being blessed?" "How is God being glorified?" or "How is God being exalted?" As a result, what was being subtly communicated was that it is all about us! We are what God died for and lives for. It was Cat Theology coming from the main speaker in front of twenty thousand people.

You can hear incomplete Cat Theology and incomplete teaching on Christian radio and from the pulpit. Have you heard the analogy of the bird in the birdcage? The story involves a bird feeling cooped up in a cage. The bird is feeling cramped, and it wants to fly. It wants to spread its wings and be free. But little does the bird know that there's a cat right outside the cage waiting to grab it. The moral of the story is that the bird needs to stay inside the cage for its own good.

The lesson is supposed to be an analogy of the way many Christians feel cooped up in the laws and desires of God. As a result, they think it's not fair to have to abide within those restrictions. But, just as the bird was safe in the cage, we are safe within God's laws, which were written for our protection.

Although the above teaching is true, it is incomplete. Could it ever be that God would allow the bird to be killed by the cat? "No," we cry, "that would never happen." Why? We never tend to think about it from the cat's perspective. We like to think it is all about the bird (us). God would never want any hardship or harm to come to us. Cats have therefore failed to apply Dog Theology to the times when God allowed Paul to be beaten multiple times, Stephen to be stoned to death, or multitudes of Christians to be martyred for His glory.

Did you notice that when we talk about martyrdom, we talk about it in terms of God's glory? But when we talk about God's blessings, we rarely mention them in the context of His glory. We just focus in on the blessings.

Implications

This has direct implications on how we pray for our nation. Cats want God to bless America for America's sake. They envision a better economy with bigger homes and lower interest rates, where the taxes are few and the gas is cheap.

Dogs want God to bless America not only for the above reasons but also so that America might be one of the greatest exporters of His glory to all the nations of the earth. Dogs are constantly envisioning a better economy so short-term mission teams have the money to go to the ends of the earth, where finances can be raised up to help the JESUS film get into places where the gospel hasn't been heard, where long-term missionaries can raise their full support in under a year's time, where Third World missions can get a boost from America's churches to send their laborers out fully supported, and where politicians live holy lifestyles so that Christianity's reputation is held in high honor. This is how Dogs pray for America.

Surely by now you've heard of the book, if not read, *The Prayer of Jabez.*[4] Having sold millions, it has been a bestseller. Bruce Wilkinson is the author. His heart is that of a Dog. He wrote it for the specific purpose of getting many Christians to ask God to bless their lives and their ministries so that the gospel would get out to the ends of the earth. He is a Dog through and through.

Unfortunately, it is being read by Cats. People are asking God not for greater ministry opportunities but for larger homes, bigger raises, and nicer cars. They have missed that God's blessings are for a purpose: to reflect His glory, to make Him famous, and to be a blessing to people of every tongue, every tribe, and every nation. We have to see beyond the blessings and look into the reasons behind them! Romans 11:36 sums it up completely: "For from him and through him and to him are *all* things. To him be the glory forever! Amen" (emphasis added). How many things? All! Not most. Not lots. Not the vast majority of, but all! Now *that's* the way to see a blessing!

Think of the two lessons (the one we know and the one we often miss) as two rails of a railroad track. One rail we'll call "The Blessings" (which we are all familiar with), the other rail we'll call "Being a Blessing" (which most Christians usually miss).

Which rail would the Cat be found walking on? That's right, the rail marked "The Blessings." They love the blessings of God and stay focused on them, but stop there. Where would you find the Dog walking? Think it through before you answer because the answer might surprise you. The Dog would be walking on both rails. Dogs enjoy the blessings and are a blessing.

Make sure you are clear on this point: Dog theology is *not* the absence of Cat Theology, rather it is the completion of it!

Don't think that a "Dog Church" is so solely focused on God that humanity gets totally lost in it. No. Not letting people know of God's love for them and the blessings that He has for them is, in and of itself, an incomplete theology as well. A healthy "Dog Church" would have many lessons and passages on God's love and blessings. The difference is that they wouldn't stop there. They would go further and talk about revealing God's glory by blessings others in the process as well.

4

What's Different about a Dog?

"Sir, your kosher meal is here," the flight attendant said.
"What?" I said puzzled. "I didn't order a kosher meal . . ."
And then I looked to my left. Jeff Liverman (one of my best
friends) was holding his laugh as hard as he could. He had
ordered me a kosher meal since we were on the same flight
home and simply wanted to get me one more time!

Months later, I got him back. Together we were speaking
in Columbus, Ohio, at a church's missions conference. There,
my other best friend (Chip Weiant) was the CEO of a German
family restaurant known for its cream puffs! I told Jeff he had
to try these out because they were so good.

Finally the meal came. We finished our main course and
ordered cream puffs. Three identical puffs were put on the table
for us. Little did Jeff know that I had asked Chip to have one
of his employees heavily mix one of them with salt! The puffs
made it to their right destination, and the moment came.

Jeff got a small bite on his spoon and lifted it to his mouth.
Chip stopped him. "Jeff," he said, "these are world renown."
Jeff then got a bigger bite and placed it entirely in his mouth.

Chip asked, "What do you think?"

Jeff answered politely, with food still in his mouth, "It's . . . um . . . good."

I then got Jeff's attention and said, "Kosher, isn't it?" Upon hearing that, Jeff jumped up, slammed his hands on the table, and spit it into a napkin. He knew he had been had!

Three cream puffs, one was different. Three people sitting in a church—they all look alike. They all act alike. But one can be very different depending on his heart attitude, depending on whom he believes the Bible is all about.

Dogs know that God is the main character of the Bible, and they see how Jesus honored His Father. They know that Jesus lived for the Father's glory; and therefore, they should too. The Scriptures tell us that Jesus not only continually pointed to the Father's glory, but also He died primarily for the Father's glory. Look at John 12:27–28. Jesus was thinking about the pain of the cross. He says: "Now my heart is troubled, and what shall I say? 'Father, save me from this hour'? No, it was for this very reason I came to this hour. Father, . . ."

Wait! Before we read what comes next, remember, it is in the context of the pain, agony, and suffering He is going to endure. This is no insignificant time, especially because He is totally focused on *why* He has to suffer. Here He gives the ultimate reason He is going to go through the coming agony. What does He say?

To emphasize what is being said in this passage, it helps to look at what this text does *not* say. Notice it doesn't say, "Father, save these kind, wonderful, worthy people from hell; they don't deserve it!" Why? That isn't Christ's primary focus as He faces the cross. Some readers may respond, "If He didn't say that, if He wasn't focused on us, then what was His focus?" Listen in again as we read His next words: "Father, *glorify your name!*" (John 12:28, emphasis added).

Now Jesus died for us and He died for the Father's glory. Which one takes priority? In this passage, Jesus seems to give us His answer. He is focused primarily on His Father's glory. His Father's glory is the highest priority. Oh, how Cats hate to hear those words, and how comfortable Dogs are with hearing them! Christ *does* love us. Never doubt your childhood memories of singing, "Jesus loves me, this I know, for the Bible tells me so," but we suggest that His love for us is *secondary* to living for His Father's glory.

Unfortunately, too many top Christian songs miss the point theologically when they basically say, "We are the only things Jesus thought about when He went to the cross." No! When He went to the cross, He did so primarily for the glory of His Father.

Have you considered that this great desire to glorify His Father is the reason why He desires to answer our prayers? "I thought He did it because He wants to bless us," Cats think. That answer is not incorrect, but it is incomplete. Dogs know the deeper answer. In John 14:13, the Scriptures point us to why Jesus delights in answering our prayers. Let's listen in as He speaks to His followers: "And I will do whatever you ask in my name, *so that the Son may bring glory to the Father*" (emphasis added).

Jesus wants to answer our prayers so that His Father will be glorified. Jesus has a passion to see His Father exalted, to see His Father lifted up and praised. Jesus did His work for the glory of the Father. In His prayer of John 17:4, Christ says: "*I have brought you glory on earth* by completing the work you gave me to do" (emphasis added). Christ did His work to bring His Father glory.

Defining Glory

Glory, just what is it? While we all have a good idea of what it means or at least something that comes to mind when we mention the word, it is hard to give an adequate definition of glory. And if we don't know what it is, how can we discuss it?

We liken the challenge of defining glory to dissecting a frog. True, you can learn more about the frog by dissecting it, but in the end, the frog dies! Like defining love, you can give it words, but in doing so, it loses much of the emotion that makes love what it is. In the same way, we can strive to define the glory of God, but in doing so, we may be missing the fullness, the majesty, and mystery of what it is all about. Acknowledging the dangers and risk, let's try to move ahead, without killing it!

Throughout the Bible there are descriptions of God's glory made visible and evident. God's glory was often associated with a glorious shining or brilliant light that is referred to as the *shekinah* glory of God. It appeared when the Old Testament tabernacle was dedicated and again when the permanent temple was dedicated. It was shown in the New Testament when the angels announced the birth of Jesus; "the glory of the Lord shone around them" (Luke 2:9). God's glory was obvious to the disciples when Jesus was transfigured and to Paul when Jesus appeared to him on the road to Dasmascus. This kind of glory is a display of the presence of God. This is what Moses wanted to see, but God said it was not possible to see His glory in its fullness and live (Exodus 33:18).

If you are feeling a little disappointed that you have not experienced God's glory, be patient. The opportunity will come. The book of Revelation tells us that in heaven there will be no need of the sun or the moon, for the glory of the Lamb will provide all the light needed (Revelation 21:23). If there is no *need* of the sun or moon, can you imagine how superbly brilliant this will be? This will be a light show you won't want to miss!

Glory is manifested in the presence of God, but we also see it revealed in His creativity. This is what Psalm 19:1-2 is talking about, "The heavens declare the glory of God; the skies proclaim the work of his hands. Day after day they pour forth speech; night after night they display knowledge." By their very existence, God's creation glorifies Him and declares His glory.

We see this, not only in the heavens, but also in the beauty of a flower, in a blade of grass, in the leaves of a tree, in the nut of an avocado, in the hardness of a rock, and in the softness of a baby's skin. God is so creative and each expression of His creativity declares His glory along with the heavens. This is why we, like the Psalmist can say, "For you make me glad by your deeds, O LORD; I sing for joy at the works of your hands" (Psalm 92:4). Singing for joy at the works of His hands is a way of glorifying God.

God's character also reveals His glory. Do you remember Moses' request of the Lord in Exodus 33? He asked the Lord to show him His glory. How did the Lord respond? The text says, "And the LORD said, 'I will cause all my goodness to pass in front of you, and I will proclaim my name, the LORD, in your presence. I will have mercy on whom I will have mercy, and I will have compassion on whom I will have compassion.'"

When God speaks of His goodness, he is talking about His character. When God proclaims His name, He is talking about who He is. That is His character. When He says "I will have mercy on whom I will have mercy, compassion on whom I will have compassion," he's talking about living out or expressing His character. Moses says, "Show me your glory" and God talks about His character. God's character reveals His glory.

In light of the above, we want to define God's glory (without killing it!) in the following way:

> God's glory is defined as any revelation or expression of His excellency in His presence, creativity, and/or character.

If that is His glory, how do we glorify God? It would be nice to know since the Bible repeatedly commands us to glorify the Lord— see Psalm 34:3; Psalm 63:3; Psalm 69:30; and Psalm 86:12.

To illustrate this, let us draw your attention to the moon. According to an old song, lovers like to stroll "by the light of silvery moon." But when we think about it, we realize that the moon doesn't *give* light—it has no light of its own—it merely *reflects* the light of the sun.

It is a good analogy for what we do when we give glory to God. Just as the moon does not have light to give, we do not really have any glory to give. But, just as the moon reflects the light of the sun, we can reflect the glory of God.

When we glorify God, we are reflecting one of those three areas of God—His presence, creativity, and character—back to Him and other people in some way.

Thanking God for all of the good things He has given us reflects His glory and is a reflection of His character. Drawing a flower or designing a sky scraper reflects God's creativity in us and glorifies God. Being with someone who is hurting allows God's presence in us to be in their lives, and that glorifies God.

One of the ways I (Bob) test my teaching, is to see if a child can understand it. I tend to learn more from the children's sermon than from the adult sermon! Therefore I have used my kids to see if I am communicating clearly enough. I have found that if children do not understand it easily, it will not "stick" for adults. So, if the above was understandable, but you want an easier "handle" for it, let me tell you the child's version. Glorifying God means living in such a way that will make God famous!

There, simple and plain isn't it? As the subtitle of the book says, "Living Passionately for the Glory of God" simply means, living passionately to make God famous! Ask yourself these questions: How am I making God famous to my spouse? How am I making God famous to my children? How am I making God famous where I work? How am I making God famous to my classmates? How am I making God famous as a single person? How am I making God famous driving down the road?

Just as your heart knows when it's in love—without a full definition of it—your spirit will know when it is worshiping God in spirit and truth, when your heart cannot contain the fullness of what it is feeling and begins to shout, "I magnify the Lord, I worship You, I bow before You and delight in You. Praise the name of God Almighty, our Lord and Savior". God will know it too. Just as when I (Gerald) make a purposeful move to be close to my wife. I only have to stare intently into her eyes and she will look back at me and say, "I know," even though I did not say a word. In that same way, God will know when your heart is full, your spirit is brimming over, your mind is so focused, and your words too inadequate to express, reflect, or radiate His goodness—when all you can say is "glory!" God will know what's really inside, and He will accept your worship and praise. At that moment, you *will* have glorified Him!

"Jealous God Ministries"

The ministry of UnveilinGLORY has not always gone by this name. The original name of our ministry was "Destination 2000," but when the new millennium came, the "expiration date" or "shelf-life" of that name expired. At that time, we began to look for a new name for the ministry. We considered everything we could imagine in trying to find the right name. We finally came up with the name "Jealous God Ministries." (The name was based on Exodus 20:5: "You shall not bow down to them or worship them; for I, the LORD your God, am a jealous God.") We thought it was a great name.

So we began to do some market research. With an e-mail list of about three hundred names, we asked the question, "What do you think of the name 'Jealous God Ministries'?" Nine out of ten said it was a terrible name. Even some mature Christians just didn't care for the thought of it. We reminded them that it had a biblical reference; they didn't care. They said this because of the negative connotations that the word "jealous" carries with it. Even though it came directly from the second commandment, most people said, "Don't name it that!" They assumed all jealousy is wrong. Why such a negative reaction? Usually whenever jealousy is talked about, there are negative connotations surrounding it. Cain was jealous of Abel, and a murder resulted. Tonya Harding was jealous of Nancy Kerrigan, and a crime resulted. John Hinkley Jr. was jealous for Jodie Foster's attention, and an assassination on President Reagan was attempted. Whenever we hear about jealousy in the news, it is negative. Could there be a positive jealousy? No way.

But there *can* be a positive jealousy. Paul writes in 2 Corinthians 11:2: "I am jealous for you with a godly jealousy." There can be a good, healthy, godly jealousy. But is it okay for God to be jealous for God? Cats fight the idea. Dogs know it is scriptural, and without it, nothing would make sense!

Do you remember a few paragraphs back when Jesus was thinking about all of the pain and suffering He had to go through, and He said, "Father, glorify your name"? Well in the very next verse, God responds to His Son. Now, before we look at what He says, think through what you think He might say. Cats would guess that He says something like, "Son, I appreciate your wanting to glorify Me, but I don't need all that attention, so let's focus on *them*." But that's not what the Father says. Look at how He responds: "Then a voice came from heaven, 'I have glorified it [My name], and will glorify it again'" (John 12:28).

God is saying, "You're right, Son, it's about Me. When the crown of thorns is placed upon Your head, the nails are driven into Your hands, and the spear thrust into Your side, when Your lifeless body is taken from the cross and placed into the tomb, it's about My glory shining and radiating throughout all creation." God, the Father, is jealous for His own name.

When they first hear that, deep down inside, Cats want to cry out, "No, that's not right. God can't be jealous for Himself. That just can't be!" Cats tend to assume that God must be on some kind of ego trip if He is jealous for Himself. Perhaps God is up in heaven and just feels bad. He is being self-centered and having a bad day. They might be wondering, "Does God have a poor self-image? Is God brooding in the heavens, waiting for someone to praise Him?"

How can God be jealous in a good way? In order to understand this, we need to ask a simple question, and that is, Whom does God live for? Can you imagine God walking the streets of gold, scratching His chin, and asking Himself, "Whom should I live for? Hmmm, I've got a lot to offer. What should I point to, lift up, exalt, and glorify?" Think through it quickly. What could God's options be? Knowing there could be a multitude of answers, we'd like to suggest four: creation, the angels, humanity, and Himself. Let's think through those.

All of creation is temporal. It exists for a time but will be gone someday (2 Peter 3:10). So why would an eternal God live for something temporal? That just doesn't make sense. So strike that one off the list as a possible option.

The second option is angels. Why doesn't He live for the angels? (There's nothing in the Rule Book that says Christ couldn't have forgiven Satan's sin along with the other fallen angels.) Well, there's been no sign of repentance, and the Scriptures tell us there never will be. But the Bible does tell us that Satan came to kill, steal, and destroy (John 10:10). So that doesn't look like a very good option.

What is the third option? Well there's humanity, mankind, people. Why not live for us? Cats say, "Yes, that makes sense. Christ left his Father's glory, and He came down to the earth to die an agonizing death for us. Since He died for us, He must live for us! It must be about us!" But Dogs challenge that and ask, "What does the Bible say about us that shows we are worth living for?" A quick glance at Mark 7 tells us: "What comes out of a man is what makes him 'unclean.' For from within, out of men's hearts, come evil thoughts, sexual immorality, theft, murder, adultery, greed, malice, deceit, lewdness, envy, slander, arrogance and folly. All these evils come from inside and make a man 'unclean'" (Mark 7:20–23).

Let's be honest. Are we worth living for? Dogs realize that in our condition alone, we are not worthy and not worth living for. We've seen that creation isn't worthy—it's temporal. We've seen that the angels aren't worthy—they've fallen with no sign of repentance. We've seen that mankind isn't worthy—we're sinful. So what's left for God to live for? Himself. Why would God choose to live for Himself? What does He represent? The Bible refers to God in the following ways:

- the Lord of Glory
- the King of Kings
- the Great Physician
- the Righteous One
- the Shelter from the Storm
- the Architect and Builder of all things
- the Defender of widows
- the Helper of the fatherless
- the Source of eternal salvation
- the Alpha and Omega
- the Maker of all things
- the Good Shepherd
- the Great Reward
- the One who holds the keys to the gates of hell
- the God of grace
- the God of hope

- the God of love
- the God who gives endurance
- the God who blots out our transgressions
- a very present help in time of need
- an awesome God
- a faithful God
- omniscient
- omnipresent
- merciful
- the only good God

Whom would we live for if we had those four options? "Well, that's a no-brainer," someone might say. "I'd live for God because of who He is and what He does!" *Why would God be any different?* If it's a no-brainer for us, it is a no-brainer for God. God lives for God. He lives to radiate His glory in billions upon billions of different ways.

"Well," Cats counter, "then why *did* Christ die for us?" Dogs know it was for reasons that brought the Father pleasure. First, the image of God resides inside of us. It was the Father who put the image inside of us; therefore, as He redeems us, He is redeeming His image that is woven into the fabric of who we are. Second, God is fulfilling His initial purpose and plan for us: to have fellowship with Him. Third, God is expressing the very essence of who He is. He is love, and He loves His creation. He is expressing that love unconditionally. He is also full of compassion and mercy; therefore, He is living for Himself, expressing Himself and all that He stands for, and radiating His glory.

Cats have a hard time understanding that. They quickly counter and say, "God tells us not to live for ourselves, so it would be completely inappropriate if God were to live for Himself. God can't live for God!"

But Dogs know that rules that apply to creation do not necessarily apply to the Creator—in the same way that rules in your home for children do not necessarily apply to adults. A rule for a small child might be, "Don't take your cereal across the new carpet. You can't handle it. You'll make a mess of it." But no one will discipline an adult who carries a cereal bowl across the same carpet. Why? The adult can handle it without making a mess.

In the same way, we can't live for ourselves because in our sinful condition, we can't handle it; we'd make a mess of it. But God in His righteousness, grace, mercy, and love (and more) *can* live for Himself without making a mess of it. We can't live for ourselves and not sin, but God can. How can God live for Himself and not sin? He is love. And Dogs know that 1 Corinthians 13 tells us, love "does not boast, it is not proud. It is not rude, it is not self-seeking."

Cats want to fire back, "Well, if God isn't boastful, if He's not proud, if He's not rude or self-seeking, then how can God live for God?" If God is going to exalt anything that is good, He *must* exalt Himself. Anything less than Himself wouldn't be the best. No matter how good it may be, it's not the *best*. It would be unworthy. Living for Himself is God's only option, and it's *not* a contradiction. No one and nothing is "gooder" than God—it's poor grammar but great theology! When God exalts Himself, it's as if He is making the following statements:

> If there are any values that are the best for My creation, any that I want to uphold, any ideals or ethics I esteem, any principles worth living for, any power or creativity worth displaying, any standards worth setting apart—they are Mine.
>
> Therefore I will live for and protect everything that I stand for. I will exercise My power and

means "consecrated to God," which means "devoted or dedicated to the service and worship of God." Now when the Bible declares, "Holy, holy, holy is the Lord God Almighty, who was, and is, and is to come," it is actually saying that God is set apart for God (Revelation 4:8). God is devoted to the service of God and dedicated to the worship of God. God leaves no doubt in our minds that He is completely dedicated to living for His glory. He is unwilling for anything to usurp that place because everything else is something less. This is why He is a jealous God. God even calls Himself by the name "Jealous." "Do not worship any other god, for the LORD, whose name is Jealous, is a jealous God" (Exodus 34:14). He is Holy. He is set apart for Himself. God lives for Himself.

This seems to put God in a paradoxical situation. Why? In living for Himself, He is constantly living for others. Yes, that's the whole reason why He points to Himself—because He is such a giving being, such a giving God. Since He rejoices in living for others, it looks like He is not living for Himself, but He is. He is living out who He is. That's another reason why He upholds, protects, and lives for His way of life.

"So He lives for Himself because He is constantly living for others?" you're thinking. That's exactly it! God lives for Himself, expressing mercy, compassion, and unconditional love to us. You see, if God were to live for anyone or anything else, *He would*

Although the words she chose carry negative connotations, she was exactly right. It is okay for God to be self-centered. Dogs want to understand all of life in terms of God's glory. Why? Look at the texts below.

> Therefore God exalted him to the highest place
> and gave him the name that is above every name,
> that at the name of Jesus every knee should bow,
> in heaven and on earth and under the earth, and
> every tongue confess that Jesus Christ is Lord, to
> the glory of God the Father. (Philippians 2:9–11)

> For from him and through him and to him are
> all things. To him be the glory forever! Amen.
> (Romans 11:36)

Everything in life—not just in Christianity—will eventually result in glory to the Father, making Him famous! It is the glory that is the end goal; everything else is merely a means toward this consummate goal. This is how Dogs are different. They understand that God's jealousy is not contradictory, hypocritical, or the bad result of an ego problem. It makes sense when you take time to contemplate it. Dogs recognize this and are at peace with it.

5

How Are Cats Different?

Remember, it's very difficult to distinguish visually between Dog and Cat Christians. They both go to church. They both can teach Sunday school. They both want to be blessed by God and see God work. They both look and act so Christian.

So what is the difference? The difference is found in their emphases, or priorities, in life. There are many ways of talking about this. One is found in asking the simple question, Who is the main character in the Bible, God or people? Another way of asking it is, Does God exist to serve people, or do people exist to serve God? Yet another way is by asking, Is God's glory the highest priority in your life, or does living for someone or something take a higher priority? The difference is obvious, unless you are a Cat.

Suppose we stopped momentarily and asked you to read Genesis 1. It has been our experience that somewhere between verses 5 and 23, most readers become bored. Why? Many Bible readers say their boredom is a result of being familiar with the story, but the truth is there are many stories we are familiar with, but they do not bore us. Because there are many stories that are familiar but not boring, we think there must be another, deeper reason.

In thinking this through, we've come to think that most readers become bored with Genesis 1 because humanity isn't there; "they" aren't there. And if "they" aren't there, then "they" get bored! You see, humans don't get much press until chapter 3, which is when things get a little more exciting because then we have something to live for: a rescue operation! So why are we bored with Genesis 1? In the heart of a Cat, there is the belief that mankind is the main character, that the Bible is all about them; they live to make themselves famous. And when the Bible doesn't speak about them, Cats tend to be bored.

Let's look at a simple illustration that might bring this to life. When Gerald's wife, Sharon, sees that a new movie starring Sean Connery has been released, she might suggest that they go to the movies. Why? She wants to see and hear Sean Connery. And she would be quite disappointed (and bored) if he were not in every major scene, because, after all, he is the main character.

In a similar way, Cats are looking for mankind in every major scene of the Bible. They are searching for that part of the story that applies to them. They haven't been trained to look for God. They were trained to read their Bibles asking, "What am I supposed to get from this? How does this apply to my life? How is this to affect me?"

As a result of thinking they are the main characters, Cats believe God exists to serve people. And because it is all about them, they hunger more for what they can get out of Christianity than anything else. As they read the Bible and see a choice between God's glory and His blessings, they naturally want God's blessings more than His glory.

Now these choices are not overt but subtle. So if they sense God saying, "Scale back. Don't buy as big of a house. Don't get as nice of a car," they rationalize away the words by saying, "Lord,

I must have misunderstood. I saw how You blessed Abraham; I saw how You blessed David and Solomon; so, Lord, I'm going to assume You want to bless me in the same way! Therefore, in the name of Jesus, I reject Satan's attempt to prevent me from enjoying God and claim by faith this nicer car and bigger home." They end up buying the bigger house and nicer car, racking up lots of debt in the process.

When God says, "I want you to suffer for my name's sake, to make Me famous," they think, "Suffer? Suffer? No way. I'm sure God wouldn't want me to do that. He loves me." And so they do everything they can to make their lives safe, soft, and comfortable. When God's glory points them to go overseas, Cats say, "Oh Lord, You know I didn't do well in high-school Spanish. There's no way I can learn Arabic or Cantonese; so, Lord, I tell You what, I'll make You a deal. I'll tithe eleven percent; I'll work with the youth; I'll do whatever it takes; just keep me in this easy, soft, safe, and comfortable lifestyle." So they will sing about the Father's glory shining in places where it isn't, but they will never consider going there themselves.

Cats basically have a feel-good theology. Whatever God can do to make them feel good, they will embrace. Their goal of Christianity is a safe, soft, comfortable Christian life! Whatever makes them uneasy or uncomfortable, they throw out. How did this change in emphasis come about? It has everything to do with the evil one. Satan knows that life and all of creation is about God and His glory. Therefore, Satan has been trying to rob God of His glory from his very first day of rebellion, and he continues to do so through us.

Donald Barnhouse wrote a challenging book called *The Invisible War*. In it he looks at the five "I will" passages in Isaiah 14:12–14, believing them to portray Satan's rebellion. Here he basically says that Satan was taking the worship from other angelic beings and passing it on to God. Barnhouse suggests that at some point Satan must have thought, "Was there not some worthiness in himself that should be acknowledged? Here is the origin of sin."[5] Satan thought he was worthy enough to be made famous himself.

This was his downfall—he thought of robbing God of the glory that was due to the only magnificent Holy One. He is still trying to do that today. Satan's entire existence is based on trying to rob God of the glory that only He is worthy of.

In our seminar, we suggest that Satan does this by playing a card game with mankind and passing out a "deck of cards" all over the world. These cards are used to get people's focus off God and on other things. He's done pretty well in North Africa, the Middle East, and throughout Asia by scattering a card called "Islam." He did pretty well in the former Soviet Union and in China with a card called "Communism." In many tribal groups, his card is "animism." "Buddhism" has worked well too, as have other false religions. He has lots of cards he has distributed all over the world. Even in North America, he isn't doing too badly. His cards here are "materialism" and, lately, "nationalism." Other cards are "environmentalism," "sports," and "entertainment."

But what does he do with the Christians? Does he just sit back and give up on Christians and say, "Well, I did okay with the majority of humanity; I guess you just can't win them all"? No. Satan never gives up. Just imagine Satan pacing the corridors of hell, trying to figure out a way to keep Christians' eyes off the glory of God.

"Hmmm," he says to himself. "What can I do to keep these Christians from focusing on God's glory. They'll never go for straight Satan worship. False religions? No, they'll see right through that one. Hmmm, which card shall I create for them?

"I know, I'll switch their focus onto something that is *safe and close to God's heart* but take the focus off His glory! I'll make them think it's all about them! Yes, God did everything for them!

I'll blow it way out of proportion so it becomes a focus greater than the glory of God itself!" (His eerie laugh echoes through the corridors of hell.)

So what does Satan do? He calls on our natural tendency to be self-centered and creates a card that takes one of the ways that God has chosen to reveal His glory—something safe and close to God's heart, like His desire to bless us—and blows it way out of proportion.

To a Cat, the entire Christian life is all about being blessed by God. They hear, "God wants to bless you! In fact, not only that, but God did everything for *you*!"

Cats think the following:

- He died to give us the good life.

- The angels exist to serve us and take care of us.

- The church exists to meet our needs.

- God exists to take care of us and bless us.

Where is the glory of God in it? "It's there," a Cat yells out. "God gets great glory by blessing me. It's all about me! The more God blesses me, the more glory He gets!" Cats can hardly think of a scenario where God gets glory without blessing them. This is where the refined yet subtle change has taken place in a Cat's priorities. No longer is the focus on *God being glorified* through His blessings for us. But the focus becomes *us receiving* the blessings from God, and without realizing it, Cats become primary and God's glory becomes secondary. Satan's playing card has hit its mark when Cats think, "It's all about us!"

Does God want to bless us? Yes. He delights in blessing us. But He doesn't want the blessing to take priority over His glory. He wants His glory to shine through the blessings, not be overlooked. Can blessings cause us to see God's glory as secondary? Absolutely. And that is what is happening to Cat Christians all over the world. They are so caught up in God's desire to bless them that they no longer see the glory of God as their first priority. Tommy Tenney, in his book *The God Chasers,* says it this way: "Ironically, it was the father's blessing that actually 'financed' the prodigal son's trip away from the father's face."[6]

What other cards does Satan have for Christians? Well just about anything that is safe and close to God's heart. One such card is the Right-to-Life campaign. Is saving the lives of the unborn pleasing to God? Yes, of course. Can it become a higher priority than God's glory itself? Yes, just watch the newspapers. Unfortunately, something that is good and close to God's heart (saving the unborn) can become such a priority that it allows others to justify killing doctors and bombing clinics in the "name of Jesus." Does God condone such actions? No. But Satan can cause some believers to be so obsessed with one thing that it becomes the primary focus of what life is all about, and they break God's other laws.

Another such card can be a Cat's local church. Some Cats think the Christian life revolves around *their* church. Money is poured into the church, and the focus becomes, How can *we* get *our* church bigger and bring in more people? We're trusting God for miracles in *this* church (with no mention of all the churches down the road). A lot of time and emphasis can be given to the youth (What can *we* do to help *our* youth so they'll know and walk with Christ?), but they can end up reaching the youth and not truly getting them focused on the glory of God. The focus can become so obsessive that without realizing it, the thought of praying for the pastor and the Sunday morning service in the church down the road never crosses their minds. "Why think about praying for them?" a Cat subconsciously thinks. "They're not a part of *our* church."

You see, Dogs not only pray for their pastor and their church, but they also pray for other pastors and churches in the community. They know Christianity is about the kingdom of God, and God is represented by other churches as well. Is praying for your church on a Sunday morning wrong? No, of course not. But it could be incomplete. Cats don't pray for the other churches because they're only concerned about their own churches. Cats need to learn to become more concerned for the greater kingdom of God!

Four Sick People

Much of this self-centered communication comes to us non-verbally or subtly. We want to show you how to spot it using the following story. In 1999, a huge earthquake hit Turkey. Official reports said that eighteen thousand were killed, while thousands of others were physically hurt and many others left homeless. All week, reports were pouring in through all the news stations. It was impossible not to be aware of the earthquake and the relief efforts going on in that country.

That first Sunday after the quake was like every other Sunday throughout the year. In America, Christians got up and went to church, fully aware of what was happening in a country thousands of miles away from them. And what happened?

One particular church lifted up a prayer. But what did they pray for? Was it for the hundreds of thousands of Muslims injured, some of whom were on the brink of an eternal destiny without Christ? Was it for the millions of homeless people who needed to see the glory of God in Christian aid and relief? No. On this particular Sunday, this church prayed for the four people in their church who were in the hospital due to sickness.

Think about it. They prayed for four people in an American city with the best medical facilities, the best doctors, the best equipment whose eternal destinies were secured through the blood of Jesus Christ, while never once mentioning the situation in Turkey.

What got communicated to the people in that congregation? "It's all about us! Let's worry about our people, our youth, our buildings, our elderly, and not worry about the rest of the world. At our church, God is focused on us!"

As much as God loves us, His focus on us is for revealing that which is primary: His glory. He is focused on refining His glory in us and in seeing that glory go through us to the ends of the earth. We are a vital, significant, yet small part of that. Cats have personalized and privatized the gospel too much.

Would the leadership of that particular church say they weren't concerned for the world? No, of course not. They know and love the Lord and the world. But without realizing it, Satan's subtle deck of cards caused this church to communicate something they didn't intend to communicate at all. Remember, it is not usually what is said but what is not said. It's not incorrect; it's *incomplete*.

Let us give another example of how subtly our self-centeredness comes into play. This can be seen as Satan uses the "denominationalism" card. Christianity can become about "our denomination" attracting more people, getting bigger numbers, and having more money. It still all revolves around us!

Due to the large number of requests we receive, our seminar speakers are exposed to churches of varying denominations. At one church, someone stood up and said, "I'm so proud to be from this denomination." Dogs want to cry out, "There's nothing wrong with being associated with a denomination, but don't let your pride get in the way!"

Paul, the senior pastor of a local church in Virginia, got up in front of his entire congregation and said, "Whatever you do, when you get to heaven, don't tell God you're with the Assemblies of God. He doesn't care! What He cares about is your walk with Him." That pastor is a Dog. He understands the greater concept of the kingdom of God. It doesn't matter what denomination you've joined. What matters is whether God's glory is being displayed.

Good Works Take the Place of His Glory

Here is more evidence of how Cat Theology can interfere with our communication. We "shorthand" our communication; that is, we only say part of what we intend, assuming the listeners will fill in where necessary. When we "shorthand" our communication, it often results in shortchanging God of His glory. This happens when we assume everyone understands that we are talking about the glory of God without ever mentioning it. This should not be done. If we don't specifically mention God's glory, He rarely gets it.

I (Bob) was speaking at a seminary, and the president of the seminary got up to introduce me. Yet, before he did, he talked about his recent trip to various other churches and schools just the day before. In talking about his trip, he mentioned how many of the pastors and professors at those places were graduates from this seminary. (He didn't mention other graduates or what God was doing in other places.) Unfortunately, God's glory was never specifically mentioned. It was merely assumed that God's greater kingdom was being referenced.

Yet because God and His glory weren't mentioned at all, it inadvertently put the listeners' focus, not on God, but on the school. This communicated that they should only get excited about what is happening through them (what Cats love to do!). He didn't say that verbally, and he certainly didn't mean that, but his implied message could take on that meaning.

Would any of the students or the faculty think that? No, not consciously. Would the president say that? No, not consciously. But subconsciously, the subtle damage was done. Their focus was to be primarily on the seminary and secondarily on the kingdom of God. Shorthand communication redirects our primary attention to something other than God.

Four Hands

Another perfect example of Cat Theology is reflected in Greg Livingstone's speaking engagement back in 1980 at a large, evangelical, denominational church. At the time, fifty-two Americans were being held hostage at the American Embassy in Iran. He had been invited to speak about Islam, but instead of being asked to give the main message, he was only asked to give the missions' minute. It was a big let down, but his short message was more powerful than the sermon.

Getting up with very little introduction, he said, "How many of you are praying for the fifty-two Americans held hostage in Iran?" Four thousand people immediately raised their hands. He said, "Wow, that's great. Now let me ask you another question, and be just as honest because God is watching. How many of you are praying for the 42 million Iranians held hostage to Islam?"

Four hands slowly went up. "What," he said, "only four people? What, are you Americans first and Christians second? I thought this was a Bible-believing church," and then he sat down. (Needless to say, he was never invited back.)

But he's right. We can be Americans first and Christians second. We can be more excited about what God is doing in our denomination than what God is doing in His global kingdom. We can be so excited about what is (or isn't) happening in our church that we actually resent the revival that is taking place down the road.

It is easy to be a Cat because it involves only good and safe things, which are all close to God's heart. We wonder, "How could we ever be wrong?" In the Christian life, Cats have willingly moved the glory of God to second place in order that good things for them might be number one.

Before we go on to the next section, we want to be sure we are communicating clearly to you. Cat Theology is not *wrong*. Staying on it is wrong, and some of the application that we learn from it may be wrong, but the theology in and of itself is not wrong.

If all you've learned up until this point in your life is Cat Theology, your life hasn't been a waste. You do have more to learn and different applications to draw from the text, but it hasn't been a waste. Press on to preaching the whole gospel of Christ!

THE ELEVEN DANGERS OF CAT THEOLOGY

—

WHERE THINGS GO WRONG!

The United States' standard railroad gauge, that is, the distance between the rails, is four feet, eight and a half inches. That is an exceedingly odd number. Why four feet, eight and a half inches? Why was that gauge used? It was used because that's the way they built them in England, and English expatriates built the United States' railroads.

So now you might ask, "Okay, why did the English build them like that?" The first railroad lines in England were built by the same people who built the pre-railroad tramways, and that is the gauge they used. And why did they use that gauge? The people who built the tramways used the same patterns, templates, and tools that were used for building wagons, which used that same wheel spacing.

Now you're probably wondering, "Why did the wagons have that particularly odd spacing?" Well, if any other spacing had been used, the wagon wheels would have broken on some of the old, long-distance roads in England since that's the spacing of the wheel ruts in the roads.

So you wonder, "Who put the ruts in the roads?" The first long-distance roads in England were built by imperial Rome for its legions. The roads have been used ever since. And the ruts? It was the Roman war chariots that made the initial ruts, and everyone else had to match them out of fear that their wagons and wagon wheels would be destroyed. Since the chariots were made by Rome, they all had the same wheel spacing. And the Roman war chariots were just wide enough to accommodate the back ends of two warhorses.

Thus we have the answer to the original question: the United States' standard railroad gauge of four feet, eight and a half inches was derived from the width of the rears of two horses, which powered an imperial Roman chariot.

As ridiculous as this seems, there's more. Here is the rest of the story: When we see the space shuttle sitting on its launch pad, we see two big booster rockets attached to the sides of the main fuel tank. These are the solid rocket boosters or SRBs. Thiakol makes the SRBs in its factory in Utah.

Rumor has it that the engineers who designed the SRBs might have preferred to make them a bit fatter. But the SRBs had to be shipped by train from the factory to the launch pad. The railroad from the factory ran through a tunnel in the mountains, and the SRBs had to fit through that tunnel. The tunnel is slightly wider than the railroad track, and the track is about as wide as two horses' behinds. So the major design feature of what is arguably the world's most advanced transportation system was determined by the width of two horses' rears! (Some say that this story isn't true, but because it proves a great point, we love to use it!)

Do you see the importance of laying a proper foundation? Without it, everything else will lean in the improper direction, leading you in the wrong direction! And this is what happens when we adopt Cat Theology; it leads us somewhere. We don't realize it, but over time, we get caught up in a very self-centered theology that leads to many dangers. In the next section of the book, we want to talk about ten symptoms of Cat Theology.

1. Cats have a feel-good theology.

2. Cats read and listen selectively.

3. Cats use selective application.

4. Cats have a selective theology.

5. Cats have a winner's-circle gospel.

6. Cats think life is supposed to be fair.

7. Cats develop wrong priorities.

8. Cats pray selfish prayers.

9. Cats embrace humanism.

10. Cats rob God of His glory.

11. Cats don't live for eternity.

6
Feel-Good Theology:
Selective Reading and Listening, and Selective Application

Debby and I (Bob) love to take the kids out bike riding as a family. Because we live in the country, the roads are too narrow to safely bike on. So we usually pack both the kids and the bikes into our truck and go looking for a great neighborhood to bike in. One neighborhood near us has a lovely lake in it. It's fun to bike around it and look at the houses. One road is both the entrance and the exit—there's no other way out.

On a lovely spring day, we took the kids there. As we started out biking, I took the lead. We loved looking at the beautiful trees and lovely yards of the homes we were passing. Not really thinking much about our bearings, I went to the very back of the neighborhood and took a left. The homes down that road were also lovely. We were amazed as we commented on the style of each home and the tremendous care that had been taken in the grooming of the lawns.

Time flew by. All of a sudden, I noticed that the road we were on was attached to another road. "This is odd," I thought to myself, "I thought there was only one entrance to this community." I got excited thinking about new areas yet to be discovered. As we neared the intersection, I realized what had happened. I had been so focused on the homes that I hadn't noticed the slight turn in the road, which eventually led us in a complete loop. We had turned 180 degrees without even realizing it!

This is what happens when you are immersed in Cat Theology. You get turned around 180 degrees without realizing it. You start off focusing on God and His glory and end up going in the opposite direction, saying, "It's all about me!" This slow, 180-degree turn brings major problems with it, and often, we're not even aware of them.

Feel-Good Theology

Without realizing it, many Christians have a filtering process going on in their minds and only focus on and memorize verses that make them feel good. Like going to the refrigerator, they open up their Bibles and only take out passages that make them feel good and leave the other stuff alone. Let us demonstrate how this works.

If you were to look at some of the favorite verses that Christians memorize, you'd find out that they deal in the areas of comfort and security. Cats love to memorize passages like Psalm 103:11–13:

For as high as the heavens are above the earth,
so great is his love for those who fear him;
as far as the east is from the west,
so far has he removed our transgressions from us.
As a father has compassion on his children,
so the LORD has compassion on those who fear him.

But ask them if they've ever memorized 1 Peter 2:18, which speaks about being called to suffer. They'll answer, "No. I've been called to suffer? Are you sure?"

They love to meditate on Matthew 11:28–30:

Come to me, all you who are weary and burdened, and I will give you rest. Take my yoke upon you and learn from me, for I am gentle and humble in heart, and you will find rest for your souls. For my yoke is easy and my burden is light.

But ask them if they've meditated on Exodus 20:5, which says that God is a "jealous God" and they'll say, "No. God is jealous? Are you sure? That doesn't make sense."

They'll gladly memorize and try to act out Jeremiah 29:11-13:

For I know the plans I have for you," declares the LORD, "plans to prosper you and not to harm you, plans to give you hope and a future. Then you will call upon me and come and pray to me, and I will listen to you. You will seek me and find me when you seek me with all your heart.

But they don't know how to act out Matthew 5:23–24, which talks about reconciling differences before you have a quiet time.

They see Psalm 40:1–3 as true in their lives:

I waited patiently for the LORD;
    he turned to me and heard my cry.
He lifted me out of the slimy pit,
    out of the mud and mire;
he set my feet on a rock
    and gave me a firm place to stand.
He put a new song in my mouth,
    a hymn of praise to our God.
Many will see and fear
    and put their trust in the LORD.

But they rarely see the Great Commission of Matthew 28:18–20 as true in their lives.

They gladly pray the prayer of Jabez:

> Oh, that you would bless me and enlarge my territory! Let your hand be with me, and keep me from harm so that I will be free from pain.
> (1 Chronicles 4:10)

But never pray the prayer of Paul:

> I want to know Christ and the power of his resurrection and the fellowship of sharing in his sufferings, becoming like him in his death.
> (Philippians 3:10)

Why don't they memorize these other passages? It's simple. These don't make them feel good. And Cat Theology is a feel-good theology made up of feel-good passages. As Cats do this, they begin to selectively listen to God's teaching and miss the glory of God everywhere.

Selective Reading and Listening

You may be familiar with the phrase "God loves you and wants to bless you. God is good all the time." You've probably heard that phrase, or one similar to it, in Christian music. We believe that Satan is not too disturbed when we listen to this, sing it, or recite it. Why? There are some parts missing from this message that Satan knows are key ingredients. What's missing? God's glory is missing. If all of creation and life are to focus on His glory, where is it in that message? (Here is another example of our "shorthand" in Christian messages.) Some might respond,

"Hmm, you know, that might be true, but I heard the good part, the part that says God loves me and wants to bless me, and that is what's important!"

Let's place some strategic phrases about God's glory within the context of the original phrase and see if it makes any difference. (You'll find the original phrase in italics below.) It now reads this way:

> God displays His glory throughout all creation, from the galaxies to the garden, from light to a lion, and from a child's laughter to the roll of thunder. A thrilling expression of His glory is in the way He loves people of all nations and in the way that *God loves you and wants to bless you.*
>
> And He wants you to enjoy His glory by being in awe of the stars and smelling a rose, by basking in the warmth of the sun and learning the ways of a lion, by delighting in a child's laughter and listening to the thunder, and by being a blessing to your neighbor and other nations. His glory fills the earth as the waters fill the sea. His glory is in all things. *God is good* to let us experience and share His glory *all the time.*

Doesn't that sound different? Even though the original phrases are still there, they are now seen as a smaller part of a greater message—one of God's glory. God *is* good all the time, but He is good as He allows us to see, to know, to cherish, and to point to His *glory.* God wants our focus on His glory, but our selective listening keeps our focus on what God is doing for us.

When I (Bob) was speaking at a conference in Liberia, I had just gone over this principle. At the end, the emcee got up and started a familiar chant which goes, "God is good," and the people reply, "All the time." This was repeated two or three times, and then the emcee would reverse the order saying, "All the time," and the people would respond, "God is good."

As he was beginning this chant, I got up and put my arm around the emcee and said, "You need to be very careful when you say this because you can focus on yourself and not God's glory. Let's start a new phrase. I'll say, 'God is jealous,' and you repeat, 'All the time.' Then I'll reverse it and say, 'All the time,' and you say, 'For His glory.'" When the 250 pastors began to shout, "for His glory," you could see a change take place in the crowd. They got it. It was then that they realized it is all about God. They caught it because it changed something that was familiar to them and brought the change of focus to the front of their minds.

Do you want another example? Many of us have used or seen memory-verse cards attached to refrigerators or taped to mirrors. We see verses like Ephesians 2:6–7, "And God raised us up with Christ and seated us with him in the heavenly realms in Christ Jesus, . . ." Did you notice that isn't the whole sentence? Cats only choose to memorize the part of the sentence that is about them. It's so easy to focus on ourselves as we read God's Word. We choose verses that appeal to us, but we don't bother memorizing the parts that don't point to us. That verse continues with the words "in order that." Have you wondered what comes next? Have you paid attention to it?

With the phrase "in order that" comes the reason *why* God saved you and me. God says there is a purpose for it; there is a reason why He saved you. What is it? Why did He save us? The rest of the verse completes the thought and answers that question: "In the coming ages, he might show the incomparable riches of his grace, expressed in his kindness to us in *Christ Jesus*" (v. 7, emphasis added).

God saved you and me to show off His glory! What an amazing thought. God must have so much glory, so much grace and mercy, that He wanted to express it for all eternity. He created us so that He could shower it on us forever and ever and ever!

Now notice something in this passage. Four times God refers to Himself with "he," "his," "his," and "Christ Jesus." Four times He refers to Himself, and only once does He refer to us. Yet what do we focus in on in this passage? We focus on the "us" and say, "Praise God! It's all about us, God. You died on the cross for us, to lift us up, to seat us with Christ."

Well, He did, but it is in the context of expressing His mercy throughout the coming ages. Our selective listening and reading seems to filter out the part about God's plan to display His glory. Instead, we focus in on the part about us.

John 3:16 is another example. Did you know that Dogs and Cats read John 3:16 differently? Below is an example of how a Dog reads and translates John 3:16. (The parentheses represent what a Dog is thinking as he reflects on the passage.)

- "For God (The Alpha and Omega, the Great I AM, the Lord God Almighty)
- so loved (This God loves unconditionally? Even when you offend Him? This is amazing!)
- the world (Why us? We're so sinful from birth. We're so impure, so self-centered. Our hearts are desperately sick. Is He sure about this?)
- that he gave his one and only Son (He gave His son? His *only* son? He takes our punishment upon Himself? He's a sacrifice? But He's innocent.)
- that whoever believes in him (You mean anyone? Any man, woman, or child? A Hindu? A Muslim? A Buddhist? Any tribal person? This gives so much hope.)
- shall not perish but have eternal life." (He forgives everyone's sins? We do not have to pay for all of the bad things

we've done? We will all be righteous, pure, and holy? He is so full of mercy! He is awesome!)

Now Cats read John 3:16 as well, but Cats read and translate it with a different emphasis (set in parentheses). Here's how a Cat reads the text:

- "For God (Yeah okay, great, it's about God. Now let's get on with it.)
- so loved the world (Hey, that's us! It's about us! This is wonderful! God did everything for us!)
- that he gave his one and only Son (Yeah! Now, let me think, oh yeah, "Celebrate Jesus, celebrate." We don't have to repeat that a bunch of times, do we?)
- that whoever believes in him (Hey, that's *us* again! This is great. God is doing all this for *us*!)
- shall not perish but have eternal life." (Oh boy, eternal life. I can't wait. When I get to heaven, I hope I'm going to get a great big house, lots of acreage near a beautiful waterfall maybe; and I want lots of rooms, big rooms, and I hope we can still watch TV and play tennis and golf. I'm going to have so much fun there. What a God!)

You can obviously see a big difference. Dogs are amazed that God loves, period. It's not just that He loves them but that He loves anyone and everyone—Muslims, Buddhists, Hindus, and others. Cats are only focused on the fact that God loves them. They can't see beyond themselves.

Selective Application

The truth is, Cats rarely read, much less memorize, passages that speak of hardships in life because it doesn't make them feel good. And if they only focus in on what makes them feel good, another symptom arises. We call that "selective application."

If Cats are only reading and listening to select portions of Scripture, it makes sense that they can only apply select portions of Scripture to their lives. So out of selective reading and listening, selective application is born. In selective application, Cats only apply the parts of Scripture that speak to their own benefit, the parts of Scripture that speak of blessings. A Cat's tendency is to apply only those parts of Scripture that add to their sense of well-being.

At a leadership meeting in Arizona, some professionals were teaching the leaders of Frontiers how to become better leaders in their organization. The expert in leadership started off his introduction like this:

"Did God have a plan for Abraham's life?"
(The obvious answer was yes.)
"Did God have a plan for Moses' life?"
(The obvious answer was yes.)
"Did God have a plan for David's life?"
(The obvious answer was yes.)
"Did God have a plan for Paul's life?"
(Again, the obvious answer was yes.)
"Does God have a plan for your life?"
(The implied answer is yes!)

Someone should have raised a hand and said, "Excuse me, excuse me, it's pretty arrogant of me to think that I'm on the level of Moses. These were single individuals that God chose out of an entire nation. Here I sit with seven others who are hearing the same message; how can we all be a Moses, a David, an Abraham, or a Paul? These were individual men chosen to lead an entire nation. Is God asking all of us to relate to Moses? It would seem to be a better fit if I were to relate to some of the everyday people, maybe relating to the masses living under Egyptian captivity as slaves their entire lives."

Let's think about this situation. Ten generations lived under Egyptian captivity. (Four hundred years in captivity, divided by forty, the general length of a generation. That means there were ten generations.) And only *one* gets to go free! When Cats want to teach a lesson from this period of history, what do they focus on? They focus on the one that gets freedom and assume God wants all of us free too!

Dog Theology begs us to raise other questions: Did God love the other generations in slavery? "Absolutely!" you say. Did God have a plan for their lives? "Definitely," you respond. What was God's plan for their lives? (Cats don't like this part.) To be born a slave, to live as a slave, and to die as a slave was His plan for their lives. Why? It isn't about them; it is about His purposes. One of the reasons was that God used their captivity to teach future generations to be kind to people from other countries living around them. Read Deuteronomy 24:18.

So why don't Cats apply to their lives the life lesson of the first nine generations? By using selective application, only the last one has something desirable for their lives. They naturally want to apply and focus on it without considering that there may be life lessons to learn from the first several generations.

Let's be honest about this. How many sermons or lessons have you heard (or given) about Egyptian captivity and freedom? How many of them focused on Moses and getting out of slavery, and how many focused on those who were born in slavery, lived in slavery, and died in slavery? Certainly we can teach the lesson of freedom from slavery. Or we can teach a very different lesson: one that says, God wants you to live, eat, breathe, and die in slavery to teach future generations a lesson. Admittedly, it won't be a big seller, but it's a valid lesson and one that probably needs to be heard and accepted. It's all about God and not us!

We're not doing the family of God any favors by only preparing them for the good, happy, and blessed events in life. Disaster, crises, sorrow, frustration, and more are each a part of life, and Cat lessons don't prepare us for them. In fact, some Cats teach that Christians are exempt from these events. If that were true, someone needs to visit the prophets, the disciples, Paul, Daniel, David, Stephen, the early saints who were martyred, and Job and tell them to get with the program!

Is either lesson wrong? No. But one is neglected (not incorrect, just _____) due to selective application. This is not the only place in the Bible where Cats have used selective application. There are lots of stories where the lessons they have chosen to teach are positive, yet there are other lessons to be learned from the same passage. For instance, why aren't we taught lessons like the following?

- Your siblings are going to sell you off as a slave so that God can use you in a foreign land (the story of Joseph).
- God might want you to marry a person from another culture just so you can bond with your in-law and show her kindness after your spouse dies (the story of Ruth).
- You are to be a prophet to the church, jailed, and you won't see fruit for most of your years of ministry (the story of Jeremiah).
- God might want our country to be invaded and devastated to get the gospel outside of it (the dispersion).
- God might want you to be thrown into a blazing fire to show His power (the story of Shadrach, Meshach, and Abednego).
- God might want you to be stoned to death (the story of Stephen).
- God might want you to be forcefully taken from your home, become the leader of another country, and then be cheated and thrown into a lions' den (the story of Daniel).

- God might want a famine to come to your land so that you might move to another country and share your faith (Abraham's first missionary journey to Egypt in Genesis 12:10).
- God might want you to become a slave to reach out to other people (the young girl in 2 Kings 5).
- God might test you by having all of your assets taken away, having your children killed, and inflicting you with severe pain (the story of Job).
- God might want you in jail to share your faith with others. He might want you beaten with rods, stoned, shipwrecked, naked, cold, hungry, and beaten with thirty-nine lashes multiple times (the story of the apostle Paul).

Why aren't we commonly taught these lessons? Frankly, they don't sell well. If they don't sell well, then, of course, church attendance would be low. With low attendance, low income results. With less money, you can't do more things for the kingdom.

The bottom line is Cat Theology is incomplete. We are missing so much. If you're honest, you'll realize that Cat Theology is spreading. It is rampant in our churches like a silent, deadly cancer.

7

Winner's-Circle Theology

If God has a purpose, can it cost us our lives? Have you ever wondered what happened to the fifty-six men who signed the Declaration of Independence? According to a story circulating on the internet, five signers were captured by the British as traitors and tortured before they died. Twelve had their homes ransacked and burned. Two lost their sons in the Revolutionary War. Another had two sons captured. Nine of the fifty-six fought in the Revolutionary War and died from wounds sustained in the war. They signed and pledged their lives, their fortunes, and their sacred honor.

What kind of men were they? Twenty-four were lawyers and jurists; eleven were merchants, nine were farmers and large-plantation owners. All were men of means, well educated, and with much to lose. But they signed the Declaration of Independence knowing full well that if they were captured, the penalty would be death.

Carter Braxton of Virginia, a wealthy planter and trader, saw his ships swept from the seas by the British navy. He sold his home and properties to pay his debts, and he died in rags.

Thomas McKeam was so hounded by the British that he was forced to move his family constantly. He served in Congress without pay, and his family was kept in hiding. His possessions were taken from him, and poverty was his reward. Vandals and soldiers also looted the properties of Dillery, Hall, Clymer, Walton,

Gwinnett, Heyward, Ruttledge, and Middleton.

At the battle of Yorktown, Thomas Nelson Jr. noted that British General Cornwallis had taken over the Nelson home for his headquarters. He quietly urged General George Washington to open fire. The home was destroyed, and Nelson died bankrupt.

Francis Lewis had his home and properties destroyed. The enemy jailed his wife, and she died within a few months. John Hart was driven from his wife's bedside as she was dying. Their thirteen children fled for their lives. His fields and his gristmill were laid waste. For more than a year, he lived in forests and caves, returning home to find his wife dead and his children vanished. A few weeks later, he died from exhaustion and a broken heart. Norris and Livingston suffered similar fates.

Such are the stories and sacrifices of the American Revolution. These were not wild-eyed, rabble-rousing ruffians. They were soft-spoken men of means and education. These men had a firm reliance on the protection of divine providence, yet they suffered and died. Did that divine providence let them down? No, not at all. God accomplished all that He wanted, and liberty was established in a new country that would reflect and spread His glory. God's goal was to accomplish this, not to save the fortunes, families, or fame of the men involved. God has other goals too, and they don't necessarily include our fame and fortune. They might, but they might not. God lives for God, and we are here to radiate His glory.

Cultural Blinders

American Cats would never think that God would ask any believer to suffer like that because they interpret the Scriptures while wearing "cultural blinders;" that is, they interpret the Scriptures only in light of the past forty to sixty years of American history. Let's do a quick rundown of what has happened in those years.

We have put men on the moon. We have built planes that can take hundreds of people around the world within twenty-four hours. We have seen the fall of the Soviet Union and won a war in the Gulf. Desktop and laptop computers are commonplace. Cell phones are now used by high schoolers. And throughout much of this, we have had a bullish stock market that has increased much of America's wealth. Sure there have been exceptions (the terrorist acts of September 11, 2001, being one of them), but basically things have gone well.

What do we learn, without even realizing it, from our recent track record? In light of technological advances, we can dream up and make anything. With our enemies defeated, we always expect to come out on top. Our bullish stock market has taught us to only expect the best. As a result, whether we like it or not, Cats *always* relate to the winner, the victor, and the champion in the Scriptures.

And Cats, like the fastest horse at the end of a race, expect to be in the winner's circle. They always relate to the major character; they never relate to the minor characters—those aren't the famous ones. They want and expect life to be safe, soft, easy, comfortable, secure, and they expect to always come out on top. They believe that's just what God wants for all of us.

Dogs look for lessons outside the winner's circle. They also look at the minor characters. What do we mean by that? Well, let's look at a simple example: Job. You all know the story of Job. God allows Satan to take away everything he has except his life. What lesson do Cats learn from this? There are times when God is going to test you. "Wait a second," you might think to yourself, "I thought everything was supposed to be safe, soft, easy, comfortable, secure, and that I should always come out on top."

It turned out that way for Job in the end. Job doubled his possessions and got back the same number of children, thus doubling the number of his children for all eternity. But that's a Cat's winner's-circle lesson. Is there anything for Dogs to learn outside the winner's circle? Yes. You see, Dogs ask, "Why don't we ever relate to Job's kids?" "What?" you're probably saying to yourself as you read this, "Relate to Job's kids? They all died. Are you crazy?"

That's the whole point. Why do we always relate to the one who comes out alive in the end? Why do we always relate to the one who is the main character in the story? Dogs think, "Hey, we don't have to. We can relate to anyone in the text who can teach us a life lesson."

The tough question needs to be asked, Did God love Job's kids as much as Job? The obvious answer is yes. Did God have a plan for their lives? Not as obvious, but the same answer still stands, yes. What was it? To answer that, let's assume Job's kids made it to heaven (they had a godly father) and had a talk with God. The conversation might have gone something like this:

Kids: Lord, do you mind if we have a few moments with You?

Lord: Oh, of course. Absolutely!

K: Umm, Lord, we're kind of curious—why did we all die at the same time?

L: Oh, I love you all so much, and I allowed you all to come home early.

K: Lord, just why exactly did You do that?

L: I wanted to reveal My glory by teaching your father a lesson.

K: What! (they say incredulously). You took us home early just to teach our father a lesson?

L: Yes, that's right.

K: "But, God, my brothers and I had a business, and it was just starting up. It was going really well," says one. And the oldest adds, "Yes, Lord, and I was going to inherit my father's business." One daughter remarks, "Yes, Lord, and I was dating this person, and we were going to get married and have kids." Her little sister adds, "And, God, I was hoping to get married too." And another one says, "I was hoping to go into the ministry. I had all these plans." And then in unison they all say, "In the midst of all this, you wanted to teach our father a lesson? What about us?"

L: I'm sorry you're so confused. You see, it's not about you. It's about My plan and revealing My glory in a myriad of ways. And I allowed you to die early so that I could reveal My glory through your father.

K: But, Lord, it just doesn't seem fair!

L: Well, just to let you know, the way I run My creation is not based on fairness; it is based on revealing My glory. And in what I did through your father, My glory shone brightly; but here, I have something for each of you."

Then God rewards them in ways they never would have imagined! They are speechless but finally mutter some words.

K: What? We get all this?

L: Yes, I love you so much, and you played your roles so well in being a part of revealing My glory.

K: But, God, we don't deserve all this!

L: I know. But it has never been based on what you deserve either. Giving you this continues to radiate and reflect My glory, and that is what it has been about from the beginning. Some I bless with things, some I allow to be persecuted, and some I bring home early—it's all a beautiful stained-glass window revealing My *glory*.

You see, Cats only focus on God's blessings while on earth. "Where are the blessings in these seventy years that I'm alive?" they ask. Dogs realize that their lives can be in ruins for those seventy or so years, and eternity is where the Lord's glory is greatly revealed in their lives. The apostle Paul writes, "For our light and momentary troubles are achieving for us an eternal glory that far outweighs them all" (2 Corinthians 4:17). Therefore, relating to Job's kids is just as viable as relating to Job. Are there lessons outside the winner's circle in other passages?

Let's talk about David's sin of counting his fighting men in 1 Chronicles 21. Satan got David to count how many men he had.

The Lord wasn't pleased with this at all. David wanted to point to himself, his country, and his people, and he didn't want to give the Lord the glory for all the victories. (Even great men like David can be Cats sometimes and anger a jealous God.)

So what happened? The Lord killed seventy thousand men. This time it was directly initiated by the Lord, not the Lord using Satan, but the Lord. In 1 Chronicles 21:14 we read, "So the Lord sent a plague on Israel, and seventy thousand men of Israel fell dead."

What do Cats learn? Don't take pride in your numbers. Hence, churches are not to take pride in how many attend their services, how many they baptize, or how many come to Sunday school. That, believe it or not, is a winner's-circle lesson because David is still alive in the end.

What lesson is there to learn outside of the winner's-circle? A Dog also relates to the seventy thousand men who died and to their widows and children. What lesson can a Dog learn from this passage? My life may be called upon to be a sacrifice. Whether the Lord calls you to a people group who has never heard the gospel or you dying because of someone else's sin, the idea of being a sacrifice on behalf of someone else's actions is very theologically sound to a Dog.

Can you imagine the conversations David's men might have had with God?

Men: Lord, why did You bring us all home at once? We weren't even fighting a war.

Lord: David sinned.

M: What? David sinned, and we were all punished for his sin?

L: I don't see bringing you into My presence as punishment. But if you'd like to see it like that—that is what happened.

M: Oh, Lord, we're sorry. You're wonderful . . . but why didn't You take him home?

L: Because I had a greater plan for his life.

M: What about our lives?

L: I had a plan for your lives as well.

M: Well, what was it?

L: To die when David sinned, and to serve as an impetus for his repentance.

M: But, Lord, that just doesn't seem fair.

L: Well, I have never run My kingdom based on fairness.

Dogs also learn from this passage that God sometimes allows spouses to die young. (Please note, this doesn't make it any easier emotionally, but understanding God's ways brings peace and healing more quickly.) Children can realize that their moms or dads may be called on by God to serve the King in this way as well. Again, coping with the death of a loved one is never easy, but trusting in God's high purposes makes it easier to worship and thank God after it has happened.

A conversation between God and a widow of one of David's men might have gone something like this:

Wife: Lord, why did You take my husband home halfway through my life?

Lord: David sinned.

W: Why didn't You take David home?

L: Because I had a greater plan for his life.

W: But what about my life?

L: I had a plan for your life too.

W: What was it?

L: To raise your children as a widow, trusting in Me to be a Father to the fatherless, leaning on Me for all of your needs, coming to Me in your greatest times of hurt, and allowing Me to heal you. And in how you lived, My glory would be radiated brightly through you.

With Cat Theology, it is very difficult to think through the idea that God could call us (or our loved ones) home early as a part of revealing His glory. With Dog Theology, it isn't.

Do you want to learn outside the winner's circle from other texts? Another example can be found in Numbers 16. The Israelites have left Egypt, yet they are still not in the Promised Land. In this passage, some of the leaders are challenging Moses' leadership and direction. In response, Moses basically says, "If what I say is true, then these men will die an unusual death, not a normal death. If what I say is false, they will die a normal death; they will live out their years" (Numbers 16:29–30, our translation). Immediately, the earth opens, and Korah dies. But that's not all. Look more closely at what it says.

"So they moved away from the tents of Korah, Dathan and Abiram. Dathan and Abiram had come out and were standing with their wives, children, and little ones at the entrances to their tents" (Numbers 16:27). What? The wives and children died as well? That's what the text says. God took them home too. Let's imagine an infant having a conversation with God. It's one of Korah's children.

Child: Excuse me, Lord, but do You mind me asking You some questions?

God: No, I'd love to answer any questions.

C: Lord, just why exactly did we all die at such a young age?

G: Your father sinned against Me.

C: Our father sinned, and we had to die? Why us and our mother too? Why not just take our father?

G: I place a very high value on the family unit and the father's leadership in that unit; and, I wanted to give Israel a warning sign.

C: You took our lives as a warning sign?

G: That's right.

C: But that doesn't seem fair.

Do these words sound harsh: God killed them as a warning sign? Read the text that follows; we didn't just make it up. "The earth opened its mouth and swallowed them along with Korah, whose followers died when the fire devoured the 250 men. And they served as a warning sign" (Numbers 26:10).

Here is a Cat's lesson: If you are God's chosen one, then He will take care of those who challenge you. But this may be only half the lesson God has for you. Dogs learn the Cats' lesson plus something more: Wives and children may pay a price for their husband's or father's disobedience, and God places a high value on the leadership of a father and husband.

This is an important additional lesson, and it is one that can be taught from this Scripture. How this lesson would change the way wives pray for their husbands and citizens for their leaders! This could also change the way children pay attention to their father's ways. It's a lesson seen easily by those who have been through persecution and hard times, but it's a lesson most Americans miss because of Cat Theology.

Do you need another example? How about Exodus, the story of the ten plagues? The firstborn in each household died. Exodus 12:29 tells the story: "At midnight the LORD struck down all the firstborn in Egypt, from the firstborn of Pharaoh, who sat on the throne, to the firstborn of the prisoner, who was in the dungeon, and the firstborn of all the livestock as well." Who struck them down? The LORD took the firstborn.

The Cat's lesson is: Judgment comes on our tormentors. And again, while that may not be incorrect, it is incomplete. The Dog's additional lesson is: Our children may die because of our leader's sin.

You see, we always envision ourselves as relating to the Hebrews—God's chosen ones—but never to the ones who get judged. God treats all peoples equally. Yes, He rescued the Hebrews from Egyptian captivity, but He also rescued the Philistines from Caphtor and the Arameans from Kir. God loves all nations equally. (The book *Unveiled At Last* shows this so clearly in chapters four and five.) And just as the Egyptians' firstborn died in judgment, so could ours.

Do you remember what happened to the little ones when

Herod thought the Israelite king was born? He had all the Hebrew children in that region killed. God allowed the sinfulness of one man to hurt His people. Although God's love is infinite for each one of us, we've taken the gospel way too "personally." It's about God's glory; it's not about us.

There are more examples. Consider the Israelites wandering in the desert. The Israelites moved about in the desert for forty years until all those who had been adults when they left Egypt died because they had not obeyed the Lord.

A Cat's lesson is: God will bless me if I obey and trust, and He will chastise me if I don't. And, as usual, that's not incorrect, but it is incomplete. The Dog's additional lesson is: My father's sins may have consequences in my life. We can't relate to this in our culture; it's quite the opposite for us. Today everyone wants to stand alone and not be affected by anything anyone else does. But this just isn't reality. We like to imagine we can quote Cain and get by with it ("Am I my brother's keeper?"), not realizing that, in fact, we are!

Other Cultural Blinders

But it is not just America that is afflicted with cultural blinders. Other countries have their own as well. Let's look at other cultural blinders and see some other viewpoints. What if instead of looking at the past forty years of American life, we looked at life from the perspective of Christians in China. What experiences would shape their interpretations of Scripture? Perhaps persecution, jail sentences, torture, the constant fear of being found out, or the fear of being beaten. When they open the Scriptures, they have a totally different perspective of what the Word of God says. Why? Their blinders, or their cultural filtering systems, are very different from ours.

They relate to the apostle Paul's beatings and imprisonments. They relate to singing in the jail cell. They understand what it is like to be dropped in a basket outside a window to escape the authorities. They know what it is like to see innocent women and children killed for no reason. Martyrs are common. They relate to David's fighting men. They relate to the widows of the fighting men. They relate to the firstborn of Egypt who all died in the tenth plague. They constantly see themselves with their backs against the Red Sea and nowhere to run. To them, this is the norm.

Now let's not just look at Christianity in the past forty years, let's look at Christianity in any period of time and see what might have shaped Christians' cultural blinders. Let's go to the first three hundred years after Christ walked on earth. If we were to look at these born in AD 79, AD 120, AD 160, or AD 233, what would their experiences be?

All we have to do is look in *Foxe's Book of Martyrs* to find some very interesting and unnerving events, nothing at all like what we expect from God. Under Emperor Nero's reign, Christians were sewn inside wild animal skins and torn to their death by fierce dogs. Others were put in shirts stiff with wax and tied to poles in Nero's gardens where they were set on fire to provide light for his parties.[7]

Under Marcus, the cruelties of persecution were so inhumane that many who watched them shuddered with horror and were astonished at the courage of those who suffered. Some martyrs had their feet crushed in presses and were then forced to walk over thorns, nails, sharp shells, and other pointed objects.[8] Under Lucious, a woman named Ryas had boiling tar poured over her head and then was set on fire, as was her mother, Marcella, and her sister.[9]

A Christian named Julian was arrested for simply being a Christian. He was put into a leather bag with several snakes and scorpions and then thrown into the sea.[10] An evangelist named Lucien had his arms and legs tied and then stretched with pulleys until his joints dislocated. Then he was scourged with a wire whip, had boiling oil and pitch (tar) poured on his naked body, and fire applied to his sides and armpits. After these tortures, he was put back into prison where he soon died.[11]

This is what some of our brothers and sisters in Christ have gone through. Persecution has been rampant. It started when the apostle Paul, then known as Saul, approved of Stephen's death. So how did these early Christians view the Christian life? What was their life perspective? They may have instantly related to the defeated, the persecuted, and the beaten down in the Scriptures, hoping for the day in the future when they would be victors.

You and I are going to meet those people when we get to heaven, but I wonder if we will be able to relate to them at all. If you are a Cat, you won't be able to, nor will you understand why God allowed it to happen. If you are a Dog, you'll see that God allowed it because His glory shone through them, and you'll be able to compare it with how God's glory was shining through you as well. Dogs of any generation can relate to each other because they know God's glory is the common thread that not only runs through the Word of God but also throughout time!

America has only been a nation for two hundred years, yet we expect that the way we see things today is the way it is supposed to be throughout time. We want to live victoriously both now and forever. We're very egocentric to think that way. For this reason, it's rare to find martyrs in our culture. We're not willing to pay the price; we think we are, but in fact, most of us are not. We've been indoctrinated with the idea that inconvenience equals the absence of blessing and the absence of God's will in our lives. Therefore, we cannot welcome martyrdom. Cat Theology in this area has it so wrong.

But we've not always been like this. Some Americans did conclude that life was about reflecting God's glory. They lived to radiate the glory of God and make Him famous. That's why the first wave of missionaries sent out in the late 1700s and early

1800s took all their belongings in a casket. They knew that as soon as they arrived on foreign soil, they had about two years to live.

Two years was the typical life expectancy because they didn't have the advantages of modern medicine in those days. They knew they would probably die from some disease, and that is why they took all their belongings, not in luggage, but in a casket. They knew life was for the glory of God; it was not for them. They knew it could be hard, there could be persecution, there could be trials, it wouldn't be easy, and they would have an early death.

Imagine the homes of Christians during the difficult periods of history. If you were to check out Bible verses on the walls of those Christians' homes, you'd find them to be quite different, we're sure. What Bible verses would be on the walls of those who, in the first three hundred years of Christendom, went through burnings, were put in skins and tortured by wild animals, became living torches for Nero, or found themselves crushed and their bones dislocated? Maybe they would be verses like the following:

> All men will hate you because of me, but he who stands firm to the end will be saved. (Matthew 10:22)

> In fact, everyone who wants to live a godly life in Christ Jesus will be persecuted. (2 Timothy 3:12)

> In this you greatly rejoice, though now for a little while you may have had to suffer grief in all kinds of trials. These have come so that your faith—of greater worth than gold, which perishes even though refined by fire—may be proved genuine and may result in praise, glory and honor when Jesus Christ is revealed. (1 Peter 1:6–7)

Found on their walls would be verses detailing the themes of persecution, endurance, and hope in spite of trials and suffering unto death. They probably expected Christianity to be like that for all time! They probably could never have imagined a country like America where it is safe and comfortable to follow Christ.

Note the stark contrast between those verses and the ones we are so familiar with in our homes. Ours tend to deal with blessings, favor, and victory in the present time. Theirs dealt with survival and hope for the future in spite of current distress. Cats want a life of security, ease, and victory. Why? They are so used to being in the winner's circle that they always expect life to come out rosy. When it doesn't, they just can't understand what God is doing. Other nations and Christians from other periods of time read the Scriptures with entirely different sets of blinders.

Is either right or wrong? No. But we must be careful that we don't say that our culturally-blinded Cat Theology is the only gospel for all generations and all peoples. We must be constantly willing to learn from others and to see things differently. There are times when God brings peace to our land, and there are times when God allows our enemies to overtake us in judgment. There are times when individuals enjoy great honor, and there are times when some are slaves. Just because we enjoy one aspect of God's blessing, we must not think that everyone, everywhere, all the time receives the same form of blessing. Remember, blessed are those who are persecuted.

Our own cultural blinders lead us to think, "This is the way the Christian life should be for all time!" That's wrong. God has different ways of revealing and reflecting His glory. Be open to all of the ways He chooses to do this.

8

Cats Pray Selfish Prayers

China is an amazing place right now because of what God is doing! Seven thousand people are coming into God's kingdom every day! The gospel is exploding over there. On top of that, the church is being trained!

Groups are quietly going into some of the homes of the Chinese and training leaders in the basics of God's Word. These leaders are from sixteen to thirty years of age. Of these, the best evangelists are single women who walk for days to get to these meetings and then spread the message in cities, fleeing right before the secret police discover what they are doing.

But in this explosion, there has been a price. Men and women have been beaten so severely that their bones have been broken. Pastors have been put in prison for years. Some are missing and assumed to be dead. Others have been openly murdered. It hasn't been easy. God's glory has been revealed at a price.

At an international human rights conference, a house-church leader from China gave a rousing appeal to Christians world-wide to pray for the Chinese church. At the time, he was the first Chinese house-church leader to visit Western churches. During his passionate address, he related that he had spent twelve years in prison and that God had miraculously healed his legs, which had been broken in torture.

How did he ask the Western world to pray? Did he ask God to bind the Communist government so that there would be freedom of religion? Did he ask us to pray that the beatings would stop? Did he ask for the fall of the government? No. Contrary to the way Cats tend to think, he said, "Don't pray for the persecution to stop. Pray that the church will stand strong in the face of persecution."

Why would he say that? He knows that persecution can help make the church reflect God's glory in a greater way. This is their goal: to become more like Christ, not to have a safe, soft, comfortable lifestyle.

Cats want to be like Christ too, but they prefer to do it through safe, soft, comfortable means. And because of this, Cats tend to pray selfish prayers. In James 4:2–3, the Scriptures say, "You do not have, because you do not ask God. When you ask, you do not receive, because you ask with wrong motives, that you may spend what you get on your pleasures."

This sums up a Cat's prayer life. Cats focus on what they can get, using prayer to advance their agenda/kingdom (a safe, soft, comfortable lifestyle) and not to advance His agenda/kingdom (revealing His glory in all areas of life to all peoples of the world). Why is this? While they know God wants to bless them, their mistake comes in misunderstanding what the blessings are. They wrongly assume that the blessings fall solely into the following categories: getting lots of things, eliminating trouble from their lives, and having a safe, soft, comfortable life! (Remember, Cats still want to see God glorified, but it is not their highest priority.)

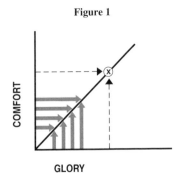

Figure 1

If we were to graph a Cat's prayer life, it would look something like Figure 1. On the left is comfort. The more the line goes up, the more comfort there is. On the right is God's glory. The more glory God gets, the more the line moves to the right. The line drawn equally between the two shows a relationship that brings equal amounts of God's glory and our comfort. In other words, when we get comfort, we give an equal amount of glory to God. We'll call that the "prayer line."

Cats assume that this is the only way God wants to answer their prayers. So their prayer line is linear. And each prayer for God's glory is a prayer that is also for greater comfort and ease in lives. But could the prayer line ever go down like Figure 2? "No," Cats want to say to themselves. It could never happen that way because they would be getting less comfort, and God would never want that. And they'll quote Scripture to back it up: Jesus died to give us an abundant life (John 10:10). By His stripes we are healed (Isaiah 53:5).

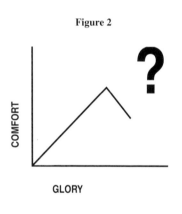

Figure 2

COMFORT

GLORY

He died to set us free (John 8:32). Jeremiah tells us that God has a plan to prosper us, not to harm us (Jeremiah 29:11). And Psalm 91 tells us that He will cover us with His wings and protect us. "These verses apply to all people all the time," they say. So, no, the prayer line could never go that way.

"But wait a minute," Dogs say. "God allowed His Son, Jesus, to suffer hardship." "That's the whole point," Cats cry. "He did it to His Son so it wouldn't have to be done to us." We have the right to expect God's blessings in our lives. We have the right to expect the prayer line to go up and never point down.

Dogs know that although a safe, soft, and comfortable life *can* point to God's glory, it is the glory that is the higher priority, not the safe, soft, comfortable life. And suffering can point to that same glory. If suffering is going to result in greater glory, then dogs yield to suffering in their lives so that the glory can shine in a greater way! Let's talk about three commonly misunderstood areas where God's glory can shine brightly: physical ailments, discipline, and suffering or persecution.

Physical Ailments

John describes a scene where the disciples engaged in a theological discussion with Jesus. It says: "As he went along, he saw a man blind from birth. His disciples asked him, 'Rabbi, who sinned, this man or his parents, that he was born blind?'" (John 9:1–2). You see, the disciples had a theological problem. They believed that sin directly causes all the suffering in the world. So how could a man be born blind? Either the man sinned in his mother's womb or his parents sinned.[12]

But Jesus had a different answer because He saw it from a different perspective. He related everything, not to sin, but to His Father's glory. To more fully understand this, remember that God has formed each of us in the womb. (Psalm 139:13–16: "For you created my inmost being; you knit me together in my mother's womb. I praise you because I am fearfully and wonderfully made; your works are wonderful, I know that full well. My frame was not hidden from you when I was made in the secret place. When I was woven together in the depths of the earth, your eyes saw my unformed body. All the days ordained for me were written in your book before one of them came to be.")

This is the same for the man born blind. God did not say, "Oops!" when he came out blind. No. He created him blind. Why? God wanted His glory to be revealed. Jesus knew this and took it directly to His Father's glory. He responded in verse 3: "'Neither this man nor his parents sinned,' said Jesus, 'but this happened so that the work of God might be displayed in his life'" (John 9:3). He was born blind for the glory of God!

Just ask yourself the question, Is God capable of healing Joni Eareckson Tada? The answer is obviously yes. But God has been gaining far more glory by leaving her paralyzed since 1967. Her paralysis will be gone when she enters eternity, but more glory is being given to our Father by her current state. Is that fair? Well, let's go back to the basics of this book. Life isn't designed to revolve around us; hence the question, Is that fair to us? isn't a valid question. Life wasn't designed to be fair. Life was designed to be a series of opportunities to point to and reveal God's glory. And Joni's experience radiates our Father's glory tremendously!

Therefore, when we look at ailments, we can ask God for healing, but we must also realize that if the ailment or infirmity will bring God more glory (either in the eyes of others or to prepare us for eternity with Him), God might choose to allow it to stay in our lives. It is the glory we need to focus on, not the ailment. The apostle Paul asked the Lord three times to take away an ailment. And how did the Lord respond? He said: "My power is made perfect in weakness" (2 Corinthians 12:9). God was basically saying, "Paul, I'll get more glory in you and through you, by you keeping this ailment in your life than if I take it away; I'm going to leave it." Yet so many Cats live with ailments and predicaments in defeat, not realizing they were given them to point to God's glory in a greater way, and that glory is being robbed from God!

Discipline

Let's look at the second area in which God's glory is not usually seen, and that is discipline. The Scriptures are very clear that those whom the Lord loves, He disciplines

(Hebrews 12:5–6).

Now if God lived for us, if His goal were to make our lives safe, soft, and comfortable, then this discipline stuff wouldn't be a part of His packaged plan. But it is a part of it because His goal is not our comfort; His goal for us is to reflect His glory. And there are times when discipline makes that happen. Again, the prayer line on the graph goes down.

Many people know of the picture of Jesus carrying a lamb on His shoulders. But few know the meaning behind it. It is found in the story "The Lamb's Broken Leg" as told by William Branham. This is an old shepherd story that was told in Jerusalem in the Holy Lands of a shepherd carrying a sheep. Another shepherd asked, "Why are you carrying it?"

"It's got a broken leg."

"How did it do that? Fall over a cliff?"

"No, I broke its leg."

The other shepherd said, "Why, you're a cruel shepherd to break that sheep's leg."

"No, I love it. It was going astray and I couldn't make it obey me. So I broke its leg so it would have to depend on me. I carry it, feed it, and stay close to it. Through this process, it will learn to depend on me, look to me, and stay with me."[13]

God's desire is to see His glory reflected perfectly through us. He sometimes needs to give us less comfort (so the prayer line goes down) in order for us to realize it is about Him. And that frees us to radiate His glory in our lives! What loving parent doesn't discipline their children when they get out of hand? This is

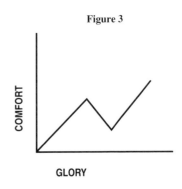

Figure 3

COMFORT

GLORY

the same as God disciplining a nation when it strays far from Him. All of this happens that we might better reflect His character in our lives and our culture. After that discipline, many times the prayer line goes back up, showing that God will give us more comfort with the greater glory (Figure 3). (But it may not.)

Suffering or Persecution

Let's look at a third way in which many Christians miss God's glory: suffering or persecution. When Jesus taught about being blessed in Matthew 5, He said something that would sound strange if the average person really stopped to think about it. He said:

> Blessed are those who are persecuted because of righteousness, for theirs is the kingdom of heaven. Blessed are you when people insult you, persecute you and falsely say all kinds of evil against you because of me. Rejoice and be glad, because great is your reward in heaven, for in the same way they persecuted the prophets who were before you. (Matthew 5:10–11)

We're blessed when we are persecuted? But persecution doesn't make our lives more comfortable; it doesn't make them easier. That's okay. Jesus is still saying that we are blessed. What this means is that there are some kinds of blessings that God wants to come our way that point the prayer line down. In winner's-circle theology, we view our heritage and how we interpret the Bible only in light of the past forty to sixty years, and, in doing so, we forget the ages past. In a similar way, we forget what God has allowed to happen to believers in previous times.

Remember, God has historically allowed tragic things to happen to His children in order to expand His kingdom and reveal His glory. We strongly suggest that you get a copy of *Foxe's Book of*

Martyrs and read it. The graphs of the martyrs in that book would look like Figure 4. Tremendous glory is given to God in times of persecution. God allows the sins of this world to work in such a way as to reveal His glory. Does God want people to be persecuted? Will there be persecution in heaven? To both questions, the answer is no. Could it have been stopped here on earth? Yes. But God knew He'd get more glory by allowing it to happen. God uses both good and evil for His glory.

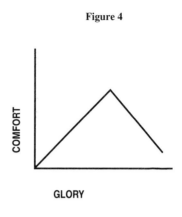

Figure 4

> You, O LORD, keep my lamp burning;
> my God *turns my darkness into light.*
> (Psalm 18:28, emphasis added)

> We sent Timothy, who is our brother and God's fellow worker in spreading the gospel of Christ, to strengthen and encourage you in your faith, so that no one would be unsettled by these trials. You know quite well that we were *destined for them.* In fact, when we were with you, we kept telling you that *we would be persecuted.*
> (1 Thessalonians 3:2–4, emphasis added)

Remember that this is not restricted to ages past, but it occurs now in other places. (Check out a persecuted Christians' web page, such as EMP.org.) But when Cats see anything happening where their prayer lines would go down (like that of a martyr), they try to help God see things their way by saying, "Look, Lord, You'd get the same amount of glory if instead of having my prayer line go down and to the right, You had it go up and to the right" (Figure 5).

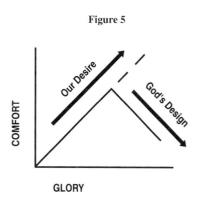

Figure 5

Little do they realize that what they are really doing is praying selfish prayers. Their graphs look something like Figure 6.

God is getting little to no glory, but they are getting tremendous comfort and security. And the sad thing is they are still saying, "Praise the Lord!" and "Isn't God great!" But in reality, they've lost the Lordship of Christ in their lives because their primary concern is for their safety and comfort. Cats can be "Christian" on the outside (praying, going to church, teaching Sunday school) but be so far from glorifying God.

Dogs don't live this way. Dogs constantly ask, "What will give God more glory?" and their prayers are geared to maximizing God's glory in their lives. If it means tough times, Dogs are aware that God often causes them in the lives of His children. But don't misunderstand us, Dogs aren't masochistic. They don't eagerly want to become martyrs, but at the same time, they don't shy away from it. It's about God's glory; it's not about us.

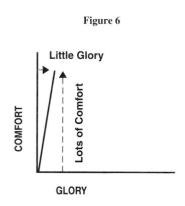

Figure 6

9

Robbing God of His Glory during Hard Times

In Sierra Leone, several courageous church-planting teams were showing The JESUS Film in an area involved in a civil war. Conditions deteriorated rapidly, and rebels overran the district. The film team had just hidden their equipment when four of their members were captured by the rebels and commandeered as slaves.

For months they were forced to carry rebel equipment and supplies from place to place. Their shoes were taken to keep them from fleeing. As they marched long distances, deep cuts opened on their bare feet. Severe infections set in, spreading up their legs. One of the team members finally approached a soldier and told him he could go no further because the pain was so great. The soldier responded by putting an AKA rifle to his head and killing him. How could God use this for His glory? And did the remaining team members still trust in God, declaring His sovereignty?

Eventually, the rebels found the hidden projection equipment and a copy of the film in their own language. They ordered the team members to set up the equipment and show the film. After watching The JESUS Film, a few of the soldiers became Christians and were so impressed that they showed it to their commander.

He in turn ordered the film to be shown to all rebels in the area! Several trusted Christ. Before being released, the "slave" film-team members became "chaplains" to the rebels and discipled them in their new-found faith.

The entire time, God had a plan. He knew what He was doing. (He always knows what He is doing.) And during all the hard times that come our way, He asks us to continually put our faith in Him because this gives Him glory.

To help us understand more about learning to give God glory during tough times, we need to talk about something called "potential glory." To understand what that is, let's think about a $100 bill. If you were offered a crisp new $100 bill, would you want it? Of course you would! (Please play the game; it helps the reading go a lot easier!) But if it were wadded up, crushed in a hand, and rolled into a small ball, would you still want it? Of course you would because it's still worth $100. And what if the $100 bill were thrown to the floor and stomped on several times, would you still want it? Again your answer would be a resounding yes, because it's value hasn't changed!

What if that $100 bill's name were used in vain, and someone was cursing and swearing with it. Would you still want it? Of course, you say again. But why? Why would you still want it? The answer is because it's still worth one hundred dollars! No matter what we do to the bill, it still retains its value. You can trample on it, you can abuse and misuse it, you can yell at it and take its name in vain; but, no matter what you do to that bill, it doesn't lose its value.

This same principle applies to God's glory. No matter what we do to God's glory, its value is always there. People may trample on it and drag it through the mud. They might repeatedly use our Lord's name in vain, but no matter what they do, God's glory never loses its value. Through dire circumstances, we may not see His glory shining, but it's still there. God's glory never loses its value or its presence. Like breaking through the clouds as you take off in an airplane on a cloudy day and realizing that the sun is still shining, God's glory shines no matter how many clouds are in our lives.

Since we were created to radiate His glory, and it can shine through any difficult situation, our goal in life should be to seek His glory through every phase and circumstance of life, even if we're taken as slaves by guerrilla forces. Cats look at difficult circumstances and excuse their reaction to it by saying, "We're only human." While this is true, God didn't call us to be human. He created us that way, and then He called us to be holy. That's a difficult thing to do, but that's our calling.

Now we want to define "potential glory" as glory that can be given to God reflecting His perfect sovereignty and honoring Him in any situation. But it can also be overlooked and not radiated back to God and therefore lost. Potential glory is all around us wherever we are, whatever we're doing, and whatever our situation or circumstance. God is always there and always at work. Scripture reminds us: "For from him and through him and to him are all things" (Romans 11:36).

How many things? All things! This includes anything from changing a baby's diaper to looking at the clouds, from driving down a road to watching your child's soccer game or ballet recital, from smelling a rose to watching a sunset, and even from being captured as a slave to dealing with a life-threatening illness. We can either correctly see it, radiate it back to God, and say, "God, you are amazing," or we can try to bear up under the circumstances, not recognizing His hand at work in our lives and not radiating it to God. We can miss the glory of God and not give Him the credit He deserves. We may overlook His activity and sovereignty as we're focused on trying to escape the difficult times. The potential opportunity for giving God glory evaporates in front of us. We call this "robbing God of potential glory."

Potential glory is lost most often through hard and difficult times—those times we don't get the safe, soft, and comfortable lifestyle we expected. These occasions provide opportunities for radiating God's glory, but we miss them. Why? The reason is that we simply haven't learned that God is Lord over Satan's "pinball games."

Satan's "pinball games"? What do we mean by that? You may remember the old pinball games that had a steel ball that rolled around the game table. As it rolled, it would strike electric posts that would make the ball careen out of control in any number of directions, thereby bumping it into another electronic post, which did the same. The ball was bumping and careening out of control. Sometimes life's situations seem like that. Life seems to run by only to bump into a circumstance that sends it careening in another direction into other situations. Life seems out of the control of God's hand and will.

This is what happened with The JESUS Film team. It looked like a worst-case scenario that God totally turned around for His glory. Yes, there was suffering in the process, but that's a small price to pay for revealing God's glory in such a significant way, not to mention that our suffering is not worthy of being compared with the rewards God will give to us (Romans 8:18). God can always use these difficult times for His glory. And they are happening all the time.

Not long ago, there was a shooting at Columbine High School. Did God cause it? No. Was there potential glory there? Yes. Not only was God's glory there, but God also used the situation to reveal His glory! When a few of the Columbine High School students went on a shooting spree, killing other students and a teacher, Cats were asking, "Where were you, God?" They didn't see that God had CNN broadcast the funerals live around the world and the gospel was heard in countries where missionaries are not allowed. Many non-Christian youths committed their lives to the Lord. Many Christian youths rededicated their lives to Christ through the "Yes, I Believe" campaign, and many churches grew closer together. God got tremendous glory through the sinful free-will acts of students who were prompted by Satan's leading.

Not long after that, another pinball hit the news. It was as if Satan said, "If I can't contain God's glory in a school, I'll do it in a church. I'll hurt those Christians where they'll feel it the most." So in Texas, in the Fort Worth area, a gunman walked into a Baptist church during a Wednesday-evening prayer service and began shooting innocent people. Again Cats were saying, "Where were You, God?" But God said, "I can use it for My glory. I can glorify Myself in this, and I will."

What few people realize is that before this tragedy occurred, the pastor, Brother Al, said, "Lord, do whatever it takes to expand this ministry." (Although God doesn't need our permission to work in our lives, let us provide a word of warning here: be very careful what you pray for—you just might get it!) After the tragic incident, God had Pastor Al appear on television on "Larry King Live" and share the gospel with a potential audience of over 200 million people (significantly more than his typical Wednesday-evening church attendance!). Again CNN broadcast the funeral, and thirty-five people in Japan (that we've heard of) gave their lives to Christ as a result. Teachers led children to Christ within the public school system. The church was flooded with e-mail asking, "How can I have your peace?" The end result? God got tremendous glory through something that otherwise would have been pure tragedy.

Cats so often miss the glory of God because they are so focused on what people are getting out of it. They see the death and heartfelt pain but never take their attention off of it and think about what God could be getting out of it. Let's take it a step further to help you understand how difficult times are pregnant with potential glory by saying, "The tougher it gets, the more glory goes to God." If we could put this on a graph it might look like Figure 7:

Figure 7

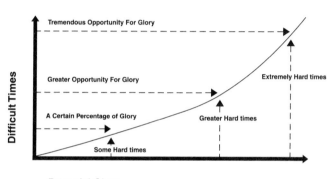

The graph shows "Difficult Times" going up. As tough circumstances come into our lives, the line moves upwards. Moving from left to right, you find "Potential Glory," that is, the degree or amount of glory that God can get. As our difficult times increase, our potential for radiating God's glory grows!

So as the graph shows, if we have a little bit of a hard time, we have the potential to give God a small degree of glory. As we have greater difficulty, we have a greater opportunity to give God greater glory. And if we have an extremely hard time, we can give God extreme glory. The greater the degree of difficulty, the greater the potential for giving our Father glory.

Although Dogs aren't out looking for hard times, when they do come, Dogs see them as opportunities to reveal more of God's glory! But when there are times that God's glory doesn't shine through more and greater blessings, how do Cats tend to respond? When there is deep emotional hurt, when there is cancer, when there is a rape, when there is an early death, then they cry, "Foul! God, that's not fair!" and are totally unaware of the potential for glorifying God. In fact, if they aren't being blessed, they think they have no reason to glorify God.

When things aren't fair for Cats, they begin to blame God for what happens. As a result, Cats get bitter toward God, resentful, and even angry at Him. Typically Cats never stop to consider that these are blessings in disguise or opportunities designed to allow them to point to God's glory in a greater way. And this is the very purpose of life! As these situations arise, Christians can reveal His glory and His supremacy by thanking Him, praising Him, and worshiping Him. But because Cats don't see it that way, potential glory is lost. Glory that could have been radiated to God is gone, and we've robbed a jealous God of His glory.

Imagine that you're driving down the road late at night, and you get a flat tire. God knew it was going to happen (that's what His sovereignty is all about). How are you going to respond? Are you going to say, "God, this is rotten timing as far as I'm concerned, but I know You're in control; I'm going to trust You and praise You for this"? (Oh, how that faith and trust in God displays His glory!) And will you begin to sing the Doxology, "Praise God from whom all blessings flow . . ."? No, most of the time we act like Cats, focusing on what we get out of it and quietly cursing the situation. And the moment we begin to do that, we are robbing God of His glory.

One woman's daughter became a quadriplegic. To take care of her daughter this woman had to change everything, quitting her job and becoming a full-time caretaker. How did this mother respond? She could have said, "Lord, this means I'm going to have to quit my job. I'm going to have to live at a lower lifestyle and take care of my daughter full time, but I know this will build character in me and make me more like You. It's going to be excruciatingly hard, but I'm going to trust You through it all. I will demonstrate to others what it means to develop the heart of a servant."

Unfortunately, she did not. She believed the lie that Satan whispered into her mind, saying it was all about her, and her life was now destroyed. So she went to a gun store, asked to see a gun, put a bullet into it, and pulled the trigger, killing herself. Here was a woman who had the opportunity of a lifetime to give glory to God by living sacrificially for someone else. But she believed Satan's lie that it was all about her, and God was robbed of glory.

Imagine a favorite water hole that kids use for swimming. One child jumps into the water headfirst and hits something just below the water level that breaks her neck. Naturally everyone concerned will call this a tragedy and even more so when they discover the child will be permanently paralyzed. We could leave the situation here and cry over the unfortunate incident for years to come, or we can look for God's glory. Is it there? Certainly it is! Just ask Joni Eareckson Tada about it.

Joni's story was made famous in a book by that name, and her fame has increased in dramatic ways through the last decade or so. But it's not really her fame but her testimony that has been so whole-heartedly received. Through her difficulties, she has continued to look to, praise, and worship the Lord. Because of this tragic set of circumstances, she developed a testimony that has been heard by millions! God's glory has been thrust into the limelight! As a result of this accident, she has been given a ministry that far surpasses anything she could have dreamed of. Joni has given God tremendous glory through it all. It's true: the greater the degree of difficulty, the greater glory God can receive.

Cassie Bernall was a young girl who was shot at Columbine

High School. Although she died, her story, her testimony, and God's glory live on. At a recent UnveilinGLORY seminar, I (Gerald) met the grandparents of Cassie (Lee and J. J. Jorgensen), who were there to say that Cassie's death not only provided an opportunity to proclaim the worth, value, and glory of God, but it has drawn them into ministry as well. These grandparents now get invited to schools all over the nation to speak to and meet students as they proclaim the value and glory of God.

When confronted with the proposition that Cassie has had more opportunity for ministry, more impact, and more influence for God's glory through her death than she might have had with her life, these sweet, loving grandparents immediately agree that her death was a tragedy, but God is receiving great glory through it!

Do you want another positive story? There was a missionary family working with Turks in Euro Asia. They were fluent in the language and were the only missionaries the Turks trusted. Then the husband (and father) was diagnosed with cancer. Although his church brought him home and gave him the best medical care possible and the best prayer coverage that they knew how to provide, the Lord saw that He would gain more glory out of this man's death than his life. This man left behind a wife and three daughters.

How did his wife respond? Did she say in anger, "Lord, here we are, giving our entire lives to You, sacrificing everything to reach out to these precious people, and now You give us this? Whose side are You on?" No. In the depth of her pain, she considered herself a privileged woman and said, "Someone has got to go and show those precious Turkish women how to raise children as a widow, and God is calling on me to do it." Right now in Turkey, there is a widow with her daughters, radiating the glory of God day after day simply because of a Dog's attitude and outlook!

But God's glory can be missed, and many times it is. There is so much glory that is not consciously and cheerfully radiated back to God, and God is robbed. All because Cats think life is all about us. We suppose life was meant to be safe, soft, easy, and comfortable. As a result, when something hard comes into our lives we cry out, "God, that's not fair!" We need to learn that life was never designed to be fair. It was designed to be a series of opportunities to reflect and radiate God's glory.

We have a choice as to how we respond to every life situation. We can argue with fate, curse God, shout how unfair it is, and wish it never happened (robbing God of His glory); or we can relinquish ourselves to God's hands and seek His glory in spite of the evil that may take place around us.

When it rains, the farmer and the city-dweller respond differently. The farmer thanks God for the rain he needed for his crops while the city dweller curses it for interfering with his plans. Outlook and attitude determine if the rain is a blessing or a curse.

In the same way, Dogs and Cats can have an opposite outlook on the events in life. Dogs have found that many events that look like curses are merely blessings in disguise. There is the potential to give God glory in every circumstance. Recognizing this is the fulfillment of your purpose in life can bring you great satisfaction, while ignoring it can fill you with great frustration. It is our prayer that you don't rob God of His glory!

10

Cats' Growth Is Stunted

One of my (Bob) wife's greatest strengths is hospitality. Debby loves to host people in our home and always makes them feel special. She does this not only for people who visit our home but also for people in our neighborhood. Wshen new neighbors move in, they soon find a plate of homemade cookies or a freshly baked pie on their doorstep. For Debby, it's a fun way of showing God's glory to others, not to mention that it is "proper etiquette."

Rules of etiquette help us treat others with respect and give us appropriate guidelines when we want to let others feel welcomed or thanked. While Debby is demonstrating etiquette when she bakes a family a pie, she does it because she wants to do that for them, not because she feels like she has to.

But sometimes, without knowing it, "proper etiquette" keeps many Cats from experiencing the fullest Christian life that they can have. Why? Well, for example, when people have you over for dinner, the most polite thing you can do is to thank them and invite them over for dinner at a later time. This form of dinner etiquette—thanking them and returning the favor—summarizes how Cats live out their Christianity. Without thinking in these terms, a Cat is basically saying, "Since Christ died on the cross for me (He did something nice for me), I should thank Him and at least live for Him (I should return the favor)." A Cat asks, "Isn't that what living for Christ with a thankful heart is all about?"

Now Cats know they can never fully pay God back, so they try to pay back whatever they can. This comes as they try to live the Christian life on their own, as best they can. Because of this, Cats don't grow to their full potential. They can't. Why? Their growth is stunted. Returning the favor takes away the power of living the Christian life.

"Help-Me" Prayers

When I (Bob) was in college, I used to type out my prayers. Many prayers went like this:

Lord, help me to be holy.

Lord, help me to love You more.

Lord, help me to be bold in sharing my faith.

Lord, help me to become more like You. (And on and on they went.)

One day as I was praying, I felt the Lord say to me, "Bob, what are you asking Me to do?"

I replied, "Lord, what do You mean? I'm asking for Your help. I can't do this on my own."

"Yes," His Spirit gently nudged me, "but what does that mean?"

"I don't get it, God," I said. "I need Your help. I can't do it without You."

"But what does that mean?" He said again.

And then it hit me like a ton of bricks! I had been asking *God* to help *me*. I was trying to return the favor of eternal life by living for God on my own power and strength. I never would have put a percentage on it, but let's say that I was trying to live 70 percent in the power of the flesh (as the Bible calls it) and was asking God to complete the other 30 percent.

And somehow (though I never would have said it) I thought

that when I got to the "heavenly Olympics" and the medals were given out, I would get the gold (after all I had done 70 percent of the work) and Christ would be standing next to me with the silver (He had helped me do the additional 30 percent of the work). And I was going to say to Him, "Thanks, Jesus, I couldn't have done it without you."

Little did I know that I was living like a Cat and that it was limiting my spiritual growth. In John 15:5 Jesus says: "I am the vine; you are the branches. If a man remains in me and I in him, he will bear much fruit; apart from me you can do *nothing*" (emphasis added). I never really understood what that "nothing" meant, especially since we can put men on the moon, we can create computers that sort through tons of information in a nanosecond, we can save premature babies—there are tons of things humans can do without acknowledging God.

But it dawned on me that it meant "nothing of eternal significance." Trying to live 70 percent of the Christian life on my own was limiting God to bringing about only 30 percent of growth in my life. He wanted me to grow more, but, like a Cat, I didn't trust Him for my growth. I thought I had to struggle for it by myself. Therefore, 70 percent of the potential spiritual growth in my life wasn't happening.

When I realized this, a passage from the Bible jumped out at me and has changed my life. It says: "A new heart also will I give you, and a new spirit will I put within you: and I will take away the stony heart out of your flesh, and I will give you an heart of flesh. And I will put my spirit within you, and *cause you* to walk in my statutes, and ye shall keep my judgments, and do them" (Ezekiel 36:26 KJV, emphasis added).

"Cause-Me" Prayers

God wants to *cause* us to walk with Him! When I realized what that verse meant, a huge burden was lifted from my shoulders. No longer was the burden of living the Christian life on my shoulders. It was on God's. He was the One who was responsible for causing me to live a life pleasing to Him. And as He provided, He would get the glory, becoming more famous in our eyes! After that, I changed my prayers. They are now like this:

Lord, cause me to be holy.

Lord, cause me to love You more.

Lord, cause me to be bold in sharing my faith.

Lord, cause me to become more like You. (And on and on they go.)

"So should we do nothing and give it all to God?" Cats ask. Dogs know that the balance between our effort and God's effort is found in Colossians 1:29. It says: "To this end I labor, struggling with all his energy, which so powerfully works in me."

The phrase "I labor" refers to us going through the motions. I've finally learned that, yes, I need to have a quiet time; yes, I need to be in God's Word; but unless God meets me there, nothing is going to happen. And if I'm not going through those motions, then God doesn't have the opportunities to cause the growth to take place. Dogs know that growth in the Christian life comes as we take steps toward giving God opportunities to make changes in our lives. If we don't give Him those opportunities, nothing will come about.

The phrase "his energy" refers to God empowering us during those times. This happens when we pray things like, "Lord, I'm going to go out and share my faith today, but unless You speak through me and touch people's hearts, nothing is going to happen," or "Lord, I'm going to have a quiet time, but unless You meet me there, it will be like dry shredded wheat." Dogs know that we go through the motions, and God brings about 100 percent of the growth and gets all the glory. This pleases a jealous God! If we don't go through the motions, then God doesn't have the opportunities to cause our growth.

Growth in All Areas of Life

I found that this applies in every area of life, even the most basic. For years I tried to "fall in love with God," not really knowing what to do. But God even wanted to work in that area of my life. Deuteronomy 30:6 says: "The LORD your God will circumcise your hearts and the hearts of your descendants, so that you may love him with all your heart and with all your soul, and live." God wants to circumcise our hearts to love Him. He will cause us to love Him. So even in the most basic areas of the Christian life, Dogs know that one of the first steps is to call on God to cause us to love Him!

This even applies to marriage. Debby is an extremely beautiful woman—that's one of the reasons I married her. I did this in part (I've come to realize later) because I had a poor self-image. I wanted other guys to look at her next to me and to say, "Wow, you've really got a babe!" But that puppy love wore off as our marriage continued. As with any couple, our marriage began to move from the honeymoon stage to the reality stage, and I began to struggle with loving her as I should.

And then I relearned the lesson all over again. I had been trying to love my wife in my own power and strength. I repented and began to pray, "Lord, cause me to love my wife the way I should." Today we have a healthy marriage, and all of the credit and glory goes to God.

This principle applies not only to the big areas of life (loving God, loving your spouse, etc.) but also to the little areas. That is another place where Cats stunt their growth. This happens in activities that Cats commonly do, when they've "been there and got the T-shirt." So they begin to rely on their own power in these little areas.

Cats begin to think things like: "I've driven to work a thousand times; I don't need God's help." "I've flown all over the world; I know nothing will happen to the plane." "I've taught this Sunday school lesson lots of times; it'll come out all right." "I've seen this problem before; I know how to handle it." "I know how to do my job; I don't need to pray about it."

The things we've done thousands of times can cause us to rely on our strength and not trust in the Lord for His power and strength. And when we do that, we're working in the power of the flesh. That doesn't please a jealous God. What does please Him, and what Dogs pray is, "Lord, I've given this talk a thousand times. You've demonstrated that You love to use it, but I'm still 100 percent dependent on You to speak through me and to change lives." "God, I'm looking to You to empower me today as I do the laundry, act as a taxi driver, go shopping, make dinner, and do the dishes." "God, I need You at the office today. I know I could do it all in my own power and strength, but I don't want to because I don't want to live my life in the power of the flesh."

Dogs know that when God has you over for dinner, there's only one response: "God, thank you. You are so very kind. Could You have me over for breakfast too?" And then when He has you over for breakfast, you say, "Lord, thanks again. Could You have me over for lunch?" And then after His faithful provision, you ask, "Lord, could You have me over for dinner?"

In America, we would wear out our welcome acting this way! But with God, it never wears out. Why? The more we come to God, the more glory He gets by providing for us day after day. God wants you to bring every aspect of your life to Him and to trust in His future empowerment.

Now I realize that when I get to the heavenly Olympics, I won't be getting any of the medals. Jesus will get the gold for 100 percent of the work, and I won't even be on the podium. All of the glory goes to God!

11

Eternity, Minus 70

One Sunday I (Gerald) used my best friend, Ken, a pair of walkie-talkies, and a very long rope to help my congregation understand the length of eternity. I asked him to take one of the walkie-talkies and the roll of rope and begin walking across the auditorium. It wasn't long before Ken was not only past the last row of seating but was out in the foyer. He looked back in and asked "How far do you want me to go?" and I replied, "Keep going until you run out of rope, and then, call me on the radio." A few moments later the radio beeped and Ken said, "I'm in the parking lot and I've got the end of the rope in my hand. What now?" I radioed back, "Get two spools of rope from my car, tie the ends together, and keep walking." As the church service continued, a little later the radio beeped again. This time Ken said he was at the street. I told him to head toward the major intersection about a block away and to call me back when he was there. The service continued until it was interrupted again by Ken announcing he was at the intersection and had enough rope to get across the road. I told him to go ahead.

In actuality, this was a living parable, for Ken was still standing in the foyer of the church, but everyone in the church had a vivid mental picture of him being at the busy intersection and where he was headed. Moments later, another call. Ken told us all that he still had plenty of rope and was now down at a local fast-food shop and was actually ordering at their walk-up window placing an order for a drink. Everyone smiled and acknowledged, "That's Ken!"

Next, I picked up my end of the rope and tied a knot about seven inches from the end and told the congregation that the seven-inch span of rope represented our 70 years of life on planet earth. The rest of the rope represented eternity. It gave a splendid illustration of the foolishness in planning your life for a mere 70 years when eternity is so indescribably long. This is also a great illustration of how a Cat plans his life and his relationship with God!

Cats put the majority of their attention and planning on gathering to themselves all the ingredients they think are necessary to make this life—this 70 years on earth—as safe, soft, easy, and comfortable as possible. Admittedly, they also give attention to the eternity, but only to be sure they arrive there! As we mentioned earlier, Cats have used Jesus as their "Fire Insurance" from hell and their "Free Pass" for Heaven, but they have taken little time to prepare for the coming relationship with God Himself.

On the other hand, Dogs are planning for eternity—the l-o-n-g haul. They know that 70 years here on this earth is nothing compared to eternity. In studying the comparison, they realize, "The life I was really created for must begin after I die!"

To a Dog, life here on this earth is like the tryouts for a team along with the pre-season. Trying out for the team is coming to know Christ. Once you're on the team (they've got a personal relationship with Christ), the pre-season begins; this is the growing and maturing process of a believer. When they die, the real season starts and they finally arrive for what they were truly created for—eternity!

What are they created for? They see that they are going to be a bride to Christ (Ephesians 5:32 and Revelation 19:7) and will rule and reign over angels (1 Corinthians 6:3). Although Dogs are basically clueless to what this means specifically, they still take it seriously and realize that it must mean something and something very significant! Consequently they must prepare for it.

Therefore dogs take seriously verses that say, "our days are like the evening shadow" (Psalm 102:11), "our lives are a mere breath, a fleeting shadow" (Psalm 144:4), and "our lives are like grass" (Psalm 103:15l). Therefore they live, as the Scriptures tell them, as "strangers and aliens" (1 Peter 2:11) during the "pre-season games" knowing that all they learn here on the earth will help them for when life *begins*!

The story Jesus told of the rich young man is so important for us to learn. Do you remember the story? A rather wealthy young man with his life before him asked Jesus what he needed to do in order to gain eternal life. Jesus told him to sell all that he had and follow Him. The price was too high for this young man to pay—he wasn't willing to give up the safe, soft, easy, and comfortable life as a payment for why he was really created. He walked away sorrowful. How sad that he was so close to the 70 years of life here that he couldn't see the length of *forever* and plan for it. He found his solace in the things of the here and now rather than in the God of the there and then.

In terms of more modern day martyrs, Jim Elliot stands out and his writings have served as words of wisdom for us. Jim was killed by the Auca Indians he went to serve, but before he died, he shared some of his visions an words of eternity. One of his more famous quotes is, "He is no fool who gives what he cannot keep to gain what he cannot lose."

Jim Elliot was looking at eternity, and he knew he couldn't lose it. He saw everything here on this earth as something he could not keep. He looked forward to the day he would have no separation from his Master. He didn't mind giving up "the good life", the things of life, or even life itself, if it meant he was able to share the heart of God.

This is what Paul wrote about in the New Testament. He said he was torn between remaining in this world and going on to be with Christ (Philippians 1:21-24). The only reason he was willing to remain here is that it was helpful to those to whom he was ministering. His real desire was to sit with Christ, to see Him as He is, and to enjoy His companionship!

In simple terms, Dogs live for eternity. Cats live for the 70 or so years here on this earth.

Let us go on record saying there is nothing wrong with preparing for life in this world or in enjoying it! God *does* love you, and the gift of life is a treasure to be enjoyed. The things of this life are often the fruit of our labor and the reward of hard work. God's word even tell us to enjoy it (1 Timothy 6:17), they are not to be denied. But their value in our eyes is never to come anywhere close to the value we prize in our Lord.

This is what God is telling us in Luke 14:26. We are to hate our father, mother, wife, children, brothers, and sisters, even our own life if we are to be a disciple of Christ. Christ is not talking about literally hating these people. Rather He is saying, your love for me should be so strong that your love for others would *look* like a hatred. This is where many Cats fall short. They enjoy people and the gifts from God far more than the God Himself.

Because their love for God isn't stronger than their love for others, Cats don't believe God when he says "Do not store up for yourselves treasures on earth, where moth and rust destroy . . . but store up for yourselves treasures in heaven" (Matthew 6:19-20). Cats are so near-sighted, they can't delay their gratification. For them, life is the season and heaven is second best—retirement!

A sign of maturity is being able to appreciate delayed gratification. A Cat's immaturity needs immediate gratification. Jesus said He was going to prepare a place for us and "if it was not so,

I would have told you"(John 14:2). In other words, this is really true. But, Cats remain short-sighted and short in their patience. They demanding their treasures now, at the expense of those to come.

God thinks in terms of eternity when He speaks and when He makes promises. In the book of Job, God promised to double all Job's possessions. He did double the amount of possessions, but when it came to Job's children, he only gave him as many as he had to start with. Did God lie? Of course not! God was looking at eternity. In eternity, Job will have all the children that died in addition to those he was given later, thereby doubling the number. If God thinks and speaks in terms of eternity, not just the short lifetime we have here, then it only makes sense for us to adopt the same perspective.

Please make no mistake about it, life is a gift and it is to be enjoyed! Remember, Cat Theology is not incorrect, it's just incomplete. When we "live for the 70" instead of both the 70 years of life here and the eternity that lies beyond, we have cheated ourselves of the greater gift and greater rewards. Without preparing and longing for the forever-to-come we will certainly have misspent the 70 years God has given us.

Eternity, minus the 70 years of this life, is a very, very long time for which we not only need to be prepared, but longing for. Life is not about the 70 or so years here on this earth. Life begins after we die! We need to prepare ourselves for that life which will last eternally.

WHEN CAT THEOLOGY GOES FROM "INCOMPLETE" TO "INCORRECT"

Up until this time we have said that Cat Theology is not incorrect, it is simply incomplete. We'd like to graphically show that to you at this point.

Remember on page 47 we talked about whether Jesus died for us or His father's glory? If we make Jesus God (which He is) and try to diagram it, it would look something like this:

But in cat theology, we take away the glory part, and have it only look like this:

This is not incorrect, it is simply incomplete. We have violated Deuteronomy 4:2 which says, "Do not add to what I command you and do not subtract from it, but keep the commands of the LORD your God that I give you." This is subtracting from God's law and is why we have the dangers that we have.

But, can Cat Theology ever move from being incomplete to incorrect? The answer is "yes." If you "overdose" on Cat Theology, your Christian theology will be wrong. When does this happen?

When mankind replaces God on the throne, the glory of God is forgotten, and we think God is at man's feet, ready and there to serve Him. Now, let us make it very clear. God never gets off

His throne, but this is the way mankind often interprets the "good news." Diagramming that would look something like this:

GOD

When this happens, Cat theology moves from being merely "incomplete" to "incorrect." The following chapters describe some of the dangers that have gone "wrong."

12

Wrong Priorities
and Selective Theology

Time was running out, and I (Gerald) was late for a theology class. I was huffing and puffing when I slid into my desk and looked up at the board to see what I had missed. There on the board was the phrase: God is NOWHERE. I began to think it was one of those liberal theological statements: God is no where. But as I listened to the class discussion, I rudely discovered that my attitude had caused me to interpret the message incorrectly. It didn't say, God is no where, but rather, God is now here.

Attitude and predisposition can cause us to look at everyday events and come to a specific, and sometimes wrong, conclusion. A Cat's Theology provides a foundation for thought that inevitably leads to setting the wrong priorities.

Typical Prayers

It was a typical Sunday school class like all the others. The lay leader started the class by asking, "Are there any prayer requests?" Then there was the uncomfortable silence. Finally someone broke the ice.

"Yes, could we pray for my aunt, please? She fell down and broke her hip this past week."

"Okay, who wants to pray for Alice's aunt, anybody? (A long pause.) Okay, thank you. Any other requests?"

"Yes, John is still struggling with leukemia. Let's not forget about him."

"Yes, thanks. Who wants to pray for John? Thank you."

"Umm, I heard that the report came back from the hospital, and Debby still has cancer. They've tried everything now. We're just hoping for a miracle."

"Who wants to pray for Debby? Thank you. And let's be sure to keep the dinners going over to her house. See Cheryl if you want to sign up. Anything else?"

"Yes. Mike's oldest son was out riding around with a bunch of friends after the football game, and well, you know how kids can be. They got a little crazy and ended up getting into an accident. His son is in the hospital. He was beat up pretty badly, but he's going to be okay. But we should still pray for him."

One by one, the requests were given. It proved beyond a shadow of a doubt that Cats and Dogs have very different priorities. You see, if in your heart you are a Cat Christian, your first thought is about yourself, your wants, your needs, and your concerns. And one of the first places it will show up is in your prayer life. Let's look at what a Cat's priorities really are.

First Priority

The first priority of a Cat is prayed loudly in churches and Sunday schools around the world. This is because the number-one priority is shared by all Cats. And that number-one priority is this: Cats want to be alive and have good health for themselves and those to whom they are emotionally attached. Really. Check it out yourself. Listen to the prayer requests in your church from the pulpit and in your Sunday school. What do you hear? You usually hear prayers for the health of those in the church. (Remember the prayers that one church prayed after Turkey's earthquake?)

This is just as true from the pulpit as it is from the lay people. In almost every church we attend, the prayers from the front are for the health of the people in the church. What are they nonverbally communicating? The highest priority is that the people in their church stay alive and have good health. This desire for life and health has taken a higher priority than the glory of God. This is wrong.

Nathan Lutz is a man I highly respect who lives in Arizona. He was my pastor for many years when Debby and I lived in Arizona. I remember having a conversation with him where he wrestled with the passion Cat Christians can have for living. He described a prayer meeting he had attended. It was for missions. The prayers were slow and laborious. It was like pulling teeth to get some of them to pray for the simplest things. And then it happened. The focus changed.

Someone broke the rules and prayed for something other than missions—someone in the church who was in the hospital and close to death. Then the prayer meeting came alive. Those who were slow to pray for advancing God's kingdom overseas had no problem going before the throne of the Almighty to beg Him to heal their friend from church. Whereas, just a few minutes earlier, it seemed like the prayer meeting was almost dead, life now overflowed. The prayers were loud, boisterous, and full of conviction.

What happened? The priority of missions (a low priority in a Cat's life) was replaced by a Cat's highest priority: the life and health of those in the church. Now, they really had something to pray about.

And what is so sad about a Cat's number-one priority is that the prayers for their lives and health rarely mention God's glory. They are not praying, "Oh Father, for the sake of Your name and for Your great reputation, heal this person. Oh Father, bring Your name great glory by taking away the cancer." No, it's all focused on the person getting healed. In their theology, they demand God's healing because they think it's all about them.

I've heard of too many people who have lost their lives to sickness because they would not go see a doctor. What was their reasoning? God was going to heal them by faith, and they didn't need a doctor or any outside help. They went before God, expecting in full faith for God to heal them. Claiming Scripture after Scripture, they presumed to know God's will.

What was really happening? They were simply living out a wrong theology that said people's lives are God's highest priority. Life is all about *them*. God would heal them because it is all about them. They expect God to give them seventy years or more. And if it doesn't happen that way, then there must have been something wrong with the faith of the person who died. They have selectively listened and selectively applied scripture for so many years that God's glory is an absent priority. Suggest the idea that God may get more glory by taking them home early, and watch for their reactions. They tend to think God would never do that.

If there is a healing, then they praise God and give Him great glory. Why? God did what He was supposed to do: He healed the person. "He is faithful," they cry. But without realizing it, what they are saying is that God is faithful to them, (not Him). He did what they expected Him to do—as if God is supposed to bow down to us. God is under no obligation to be faithful to our expectations; God is only required to be faithful to Himself, and Cats have trouble with that.

Rarely is God's glory the focal point of every area of Cats' lives. If someone dies early (and they don't blame it on the person's lack of faith), then they just shake their heads and say, "Well, I guess God's glory is in there somewhere. We can't figure it out, but all things work together for good for those who love the Lord."

One of the most balanced sermons I heard on this topic of faith healing and God's sovereignty was from Paul Goodman (who pastored a church in Mechanicsville, Virginia). Paul was giving the sermon on a very solemn occasion. Steve Watkins, a dear friend of Paul and the head deacon at their church, had come down with cancer. Rarely does a church rally behind their loved ones as much as this church did. Through the anointing of oil by the elders and through the prayers of the church members, Steve and his family were lifted up continually.

Yet God saw that bringing Steve home at the young age of forty-one (leaving behind a wife and three boys) was going to bring Him more glory than healing him. Because Steve saw God's glory as a higher priority than his own life, he was able to accept this with grace. At the funeral, Paul preached about Steve's struggle to hold on to life for his sake and his family's sake and his desire to glorify the Lord in whatever way God chose.

Dogs know that this is the balance. We have the right to ask God for healing and life, but we must also yield that right if our heavenly Father would gain more glory by taking anyone of us home early. It's about God's glory; it's not about our healing.

Many times the process (trusting God to be glorified in such an ordeal) is just as glorious as the product (the death or healing itself). But for a Cat, the glory of God isn't one of their top priorities (this is why it is incorrect). So they never give up the right to live until there is no choice left for them. They never wrestle with the apostle Paul's words "To live is Christ and to die is gain" (Philippians 1:21). In fact, Cats don't believe that verse at all.

Second Priority

So, if wanting to stay alive and be healthy is a Cat's first priority, what's the second priority? We are convinced that the number-two priority of Cats is their desire to be safe and secure. How does this work itself out in their day-to-day lives?

This security lies in the area of having good finances (a steady monthly income, a nice retirement package), insurance for disasters, and a nice home. If Cats have all of this, then they'll start to think about what they can do to serve the Lord. But note that it is *after* they get all of these things.

How do we know this? It's easy to find out. Challenge someone to go overseas and serve the Lord. How do they respond? "Do mission agencies have retirement programs? Is it safe over there? I could never raise support. I could never leave my job." Their number-two priority has been challenged, and they fight to keep it.

Also look at the "white flight" that has happened over the years in many larger cities. Churches that were the pillars of downtown areas have moved their main buildings to the suburbs. What is the reasoning? It's not safe anymore in the inner city. Hence, they need to relocate. What does it communicate nonverbally? Security is one of their top priorities!

Third Priority

If Cats have their lives and health accompanied with safety and security, Cats want more than anything else to be blessed. The goal is a safe, soft, comfortable lifestyle that honors God. (The emphasis though is on the safe, soft, comfortable part rather than on the honoring God part, but it all comes in the same sentence—that's why it's so hard to tell the difference between the cat and dog theology in all of us!)

Now many of these prayers aren't the ones asked for in Sunday school. Rarely is anyone going to get up and say, "Please join me in asking God to give me the two free Super Bowl tickets that the potato chip company is giving away. God knows what a fan I am, so could you please ask God that those two would go to me out of all the people in this country?" Or how about, "Could you please join me in trusting God for more money? We really want to get that second home on the lake. We're so close, but we need a little bit more. So please join me in this prayer."

WRONG PRIORITIES AND SELECTIVE THEOLOGY

No, those aren't the types of prayer requests that we pray out loud, but Cat spending patterns and lifestyles show that this really is how they structure their priorities. They are in it for themselves. All you need to do is go to the average white, middle or upper-middle class church and walk through the parking lot to see what kinds of cars many of them drive. Most are geared toward what they really want—comfort and ease. Now there is nothing wrong with a comfortable lifestyle and enjoying the fruit of one's labor unless it becomes a higher priority than the glory of God, which is incorrect.

To further confirm this third priority, check out Cats' social calendars. What do they do with their free time? Is it all spent on themselves, golfing, tennis, or shopping? Or do you see them running first to an international friend's home to pick them up to play golf, to play tennis, or to take them shopping and buying their friend something as well? Are they going to prayer meetings and helping out with the youth, or is the great majority of their free time spent solely on the things they want to do?

Let's also not forget to look at the square footage of our homes. This can be another indicator of what our priorities are. Size and space is something we expect, with all children "needing" their own rooms. Again, there is nothing wrong with large homes, but rarely do we hold on to them lightly, ready and willing to give them up at any time to go and serve our heavenly Father as He sends us into the world. No. Cats are primarily in this Christianity thing for themselves. God has become a great (and spiritual) means toward a Cat's goal of selfish living. No wonder Christ talked about being wary of wolves in sheep's clothing.

Fourth Priority

So what is a Cat's fourth priority? It is this: Cats believe that the local church is there only to meet their needs. In simple words, the church exists for them! This is incorrect. Cats want their felt needs to be met by the local church. They're not interested in their real needs or the real needs of the world.

Have you ever seen what often happens when a pastor sees sin in a church member's life and seeks to address it biblically by confronting the person? What do Cats do? Usually they go church shopping, looking for the next church that will satisfy them and where they can be comfortable, where they can go to church and still enjoy their sin. Why? In Cat Theology, the church is there to give them strokes, to please them, and to make them feel comfortable—not to be "judgmental."

In Cat Theology, tithing is seen as a payment for services rendered. If they like the services (i.e., what the church is doing for them and their family), then they'll attend and give a certain percentage to the church (not to the Lord). They only give to special funds if they will benefit from that project. If they have kids, they'll help pay for the swing sets. If they don't, they won't. Theirs is a quid-pro-quo relationship—they pay for what they get.

Cats would never consider giving to something outside of their local needs because it wouldn't benefit them. When the real needs of the world are exposed, Cats want to quietly and politely nap. And when the plate is passed around to give to missions, they will break their own rules of just giving to local needs but only to relieve themselves of guilt. When the church wants to equip them to minister to others, they run and complain. Why? It makes them feel too uncomfortable, and Cats don't like to get outside of their comfort zones.

Fifth Priority

Depending on what denomination you come from, a Cat's fifth priority could be the statistics of their local church, or to put it another way, the health of their local church. These Cat churches are constantly asking questions like, How many did you have in Sunday school last week? How many salvation decisions did you have last year? How many baptisms did you hold last month?

To see if this is true in your own church, just look at the weekly bulletin or check out the annual report and see what is primary. Is it all about the glory of God, or is it all about numbers? You can usually get a pretty clear idea about what really drives the church. Now is there anything wrong in having a focus on baptisms and numbers? No, not at all. But as you are well aware, it can become a god in and of itself . . . this is wrong.

In one part of greater Atlanta, there is an apartment complex where seventy-five languages are spoken. What a ministry opportunity to see our Father's glory radiate! But one missions pastor in Atlanta confessed that he was not allowed to talk about this ministry opportunity. Why? If the ministry took place on a Sunday morning, the numbers of those attending their church would go down. This would mean their church's position in the denomination wouldn't be as high.

It was pure Cat Theology at its best. They were more worried about their position in the denomination than about revealing God's glory to the lost. They would only minister to those without Christ as long as it wouldn't interfere with their standing.

Low Priorities

Somewhere on down the priority list of a Cat is the glory of God—just where, only they know. But it is usually an afterthought. After a healing or some other blessing, they glorify God (because He lived for them). After all, who wouldn't praise a God whose sole focus is their health and blessings and who made the world to revolve around them?

But if the blessings don't come or if there is no healing, then they cry out, "God, where were You?" What they are basically saying is, "God, where were You when *we* were in need?" Rarely do Cats pray about or talk about God's glory before the answer to their prayer comes. And when God doesn't work in the way they were expecting, when their prayers aren't answered in the way they were hoping, most just shake their heads and say, "I just don't get it. I know He's faithful, but I just don't get it."

Why the struggle? They expect the faithfulness of God to be focused on them, their health, their lives—God was supposed to make them famous. They have no concept that God is faithful to His glory. Only after scratching their heads for a while will they begin to think about His glory and slowly and incredulously ask, "Now, how can God get glory out of this?" And even after asking the question, they won't have a good answer. It will be something safe and scriptural like, "Well, all things work together for good for those who love the Lord," or "God will get glory through all of this somehow," or "We'll only know why when we get to heaven."

Far below the glory of God in their list of priorities is a Cat's desire for missions. Why? It requires personal involvement, and that means way too much sacrifice. Also there's usually a lot of guilt associated with it. Hence, when Cats are forced to address missions, they'll say things like, "What about all the needs of people right here?" or "Don't throw away all the talents God has given you by going overseas," or, the best one, "Why ruin their culture by changing their religion?"

Dog Priorities

Dogs, on the other hand, have a very different set of priorities. A Dog's first and foremost priority is that God would be glorified. Dogs not only have this as their first priority, but it is also their passion.

Dogs start out their prayers with words that basically communicate, "Lord, for the sake of Your great name . . ." They are constantly asking for God's glory to shine in the events taking place. Dogs also ask questions before any event that takes place like, "What will God get out of this?" or "Where is God's glory in all of this?" or "How will this make God famous?"

When Dogs are faced with a life-threatening situation, they pray confidently and very boldly, "Lord, if You are going to get more glory by taking me home early, do it." Death is not a scary thing. "Lord, if it brings You more honor and glory to take my spouse's life away so that I have to raise a family by myself—that's okay. Show me how to live."

These types of prayers aren't prayed joyously. But they are prayed from the heart with deep conviction that it is about God's glory, not about their own comfort, ease, and safety. Dogs sometimes realize that, like our Lord, they must sacrifice their own joy and pleasure for the advancement of God's kingdom. At the heart of it, Dogs have a passion for God's glory.

Now Dogs are not masochistic. They too like the blessings that Jabez prayed for, and they aren't shy about asking for them. But at the heart of it is God's glory. Before praying for a large house, Dogs are mindful of how it might be used for God's glory. So they go before God's throne, asking for a larger house "for the sake of His name."

When thinking about purchasing a tent, camper, or time share, they are motivated by the idea that days or weeks spent together as a family will result in a stronger family unit, giving their children a greater sense of security in God and in the family. So they stretch their budget, believing that God will be pleased with their motivation for the purchase.

When thinking about adding on to a church building, Dogs think secondarily about what it will mean to them and their kids. Primarily they think about the new people who will be attracted and brought into the kingdom and the new money that will be raised for missions and advancing God's kingdom.

But remember that Dogs will give up those things quickly if God's kingdom would be more advanced in some other way. If they feel led to go overseas, they'll quickly give up the large home. If they see it doing harm to God's reputation, they'll get rid of the boat, the tent, the camper, the car, and anything and everything. Dogs don't allow anything to detract from God's glory shining in and through them.

And in light of missions, contrary to Cats, Dogs realize that God's greatest glory will shine when people from every tongue, tribe, and nation are worshiping God. (For more on this subject, be sure to read *Unveiled at Last* by Bob Sjogren and *Let the Nations Be Glad* by John Piper.)[14] As a result, a Dog's highest priority is seeing God's glory go out to all the peoples of the earth.

Dogs are always open to the possibility of personally serving God overseas or supporting someone who does. But if they are called to stay home, then giving the children of their church a vision for all nations is a high priority. Asking God for laborers to go into the harvest field is a constant prayer. Sacrificial giving for the sake of other nations happens regularly. Short-term mission trips get funded. Long-term service overseas is always a possibility. Dogs can't wait to be in heaven around the throne with people from all nations!

The priorities of Dogs and Cats are very different. Priorities show up in their lifestyles, their motivations, and their thought lives. As a result of this, Dogs and Cats also pray very different prayers.

Selective Theology

Over time, wrong priorities give berth to a very selective theology. By using selective theology, Cats justify those tough passages or sticky situations by interpreting the Scriptures the way they want. Remember, this kind of reasoning is based on the premise that it's all about us. With this incorrect foundation come wrong thology.

For instance, let's take the topic of divorce. Maybe you've heard a loving someone, a mother perhaps, as she tries to comfort her son or daughter who is facing a possible divorce. "Look, if it's not working out and you're experiencing deep emotional pain, God wants you happy," she says. "So although it's not the best, go ahead and get a divorce. Just do it. God doesn't want you miserable like this."

There wasn't a word in there about God's desire or His glory; it was all about the person's happiness. Does God want people to be happy? Yes, God wants us happy, more than we could ever imagine! But He wants us happy *in* Him as we obey Him. Because we leave out the "in Him" (not incorrect, but incomplete), it moves from being incomplete to being incorrect (wanting our happiness in our spouse and not God himself.) God will not justify sin just because it makes someone happy. It is our happiness *in* Him that He is concerned about, not merely our happiness alone.

Other hot topics fit here too. Let's look at the topic of homosexuality. Some might say, "This is the way that God designed me. If God made me this way, I guess it's okay. After all, I'm going to be faithful to my partner. And what harm is really being done anyhow?"

With a people-centered theology, the answer is none. But if your focus is on the glory of God, you'd not only be getting a different answer, you'd also be asking a different set of questions. God is clear. He doesn't approve of homosexuality. That's not the way God designed humanity to work, even if it isn't harming anyone. And if God isn't pleased, it shouldn't be done. It's not about what we like or want. We must remember, everything is here for His pleasure, not ours. If it doesn't please God, don't do it, no matter how "politically correct" it looks.

These issues move from the micro (small topics in our theology) to the macro (big topics in our theology), with things like annihilation theology. Annihilation theology states that after a certain period of time, God simply annihilates those who are in hell. He's a God of love and doesn't want them to suffer for long.

The thinking behind it is this: I know I've sinned, but my sin isn't that big. Why should anyone have to pay an eternal penalty for a finite sin? Temporal sin cannot be worthy of infinite penalty. If I'm going to hell, I should just pay for a certain amount of sin, and then God probably zaps me and I no longer exist.

Note that annihilation theology focuses on people, a Cat theologian's delight! It tries to find an acceptable solution, one that doesn't give us too much discomfort yet answers the bigger question of what happens to sinners who are suffering eternally after death. Annihilation theology stems not from what God said but from Cat Theology. Cats end up saying something different from what God said.

What Cats have failed to realize is that it's not about the years of sin they may have committed in their lifetimes. It's about an eternal God who is infinitely glorious, and that glory has been rejected. Because the glory they have offended is infinite, their penalty will be eternal. Dogs focus on an eternal God with infinite glory; Cats focus on people and the sin they've committed.

Cat Theology can come up with other examples of erroneous thinking that go way beyond the Word of God. Let's look at Universalism. Universalism asks, How could a loving God send anybody to hell? He must not if He's a God of love. Therefore, everyone will get to heaven. If this is true, then there's no real need for missions. People will go to heaven anyway. If it is all about people, God is just going to let everybody into heaven! Surely God wouldn't want, or allow, anyone to suffer. (Remember, it's about people!) Cats overlook God's sense of justice.

With selective theology, Cats eliminate whatever could endanger humanity in a broad way. They rationalize it away and choose theologies that are "politically correct" and safe for them. They interpret Scripture the way they choose, and tolerance becomes the key. Make everyone happy. Why? Cats think, "It's all about us."

13

Life Is Supposed to Be Fair

Children can add such perspective to life (and give great examples to use as an introduction to the chapter of a book)! As I (Bob) am writing this book, I am at a "boot camp" for ninety children, ages seven to eighteen, who are training for an outreach program through our church. Our group, Bridge Builders, has taken over the church for one week. All ninety kids, along with many parents, are sleeping on the floors, showering outside in bathing suits in temporary showers, eating together, praying together, and worshiping together.

Every day, all ninety get trained in choreography so they can dance to songs. They then go out and perform in public places, using that as a springboard to share their faith. While we do this every year, this year there's a little difference. We've got a new leader teaching the choreography. You see, this is my kids' third year, and they know what to expect. Last year my two older ones were kept out of dancing to certain songs because of their age. It was only for the older kids. All last year we kept hearing, "But that's not fair. We can do it just as well." They were pretty much correct, but those were the rules.

But now they are older. They came with a new perspective. Yes, this year things were going to be different because they were going to be needed in every song. But a snag came up.

James, this year's choreographer, is new to Bridge Builders. He doesn't know the "rules," and he doesn't need to. He has his own rules. And his rules say but all kids of all ages are going to dance in these songs. Now my older kids are saying the same thing as last year to a different tune. "Hey, that's not fair! We had to wait; they should too." What wasn't fair last year (because they couldn't have it) should now be the rule (because now they're included)!

My kids go through a lot of anguish because of one simple principle. They think life is supposed to be fair. They got this from the Cat Theology around them. This is another one of its great dangers, which is incorrect. Cats always think life is supposed to be fair. When it's not, when they encounter the traumas of daily life, they cry out, "Oh, but that's not fair, God."

Is God Fair?

To gain greater insight and understanding into this troublesome situation, we're going to look at three case studies of people in the Bible who encountered various ways of revealing God's glory: the first is Jabez, whose story is told in 1 Chronicles 4:10, (the now-famous book entitled *The Prayer of Jabez* is based on this passage); the second is a nameless young girl found in 2 Kings 5:1–15; and the third is Stephen, who is probably more familiar. His story is found in Acts 6–7.

Let's look at our first case study. We don't know much about Jabez. The Bible only records a short mention of his birth and a prayer he prayed. The paragraph given to his story tells us Jabez cried out to God, "Oh, that you would bless me and enlarge my territory! Let your hand be with me, and keep me from harm so that I will be free from pain" (1 Chronicles 4:10).

As we analyze his prayer, we find it's made up of five simple requests, not unlike the ones that we may pray.

1. Bless me.

2. Enlarge my territory.

3. May Your hand be with me.

4. Keep me from harm.

5. I want zero pain.

How does God respond to this? After all we've talked about so far, this sounds like a prime example of a Cat's "It's–all–about–me" prayer. So how does God deal with this man? Does He say, "Hey buddy, buck up. I'm going to send My Son to the cross where He'll endure great pain. He's going to have nails driven through His hands and feet. He's going to be crowned with thorns, whipped and lashed until blood is coming out of His back, and He's going to sweat blood. Remember this: All who desire to be godly and live godly lives will be persecuted. You need to get used to that, so toughen up. Learn to bear your own cross!"

He could have said that, but He didn't. As we read on, we find that God granted his request. He what? He granted his request? Yes, you read that right. (You probably already knew that because, odds are, you've read *The Prayer of Jabez*). God, in essence, said, "You've got it, the whole nine yards. It's yours, and I want you to have it!" (Nowhere in this book have we said, "God doesn't want to bless you." We're only cautioning against focusing on the idea that God lives for you and lives to bless you, as though that were a higher priority than radiating His own glory.)

Next, let's move on to our second character. We don't know her name, so we'll have to be satisfied with just calling her a young girl. Her story is found in 2 Kings 5. As we begin reading, we need to be aware of the context. This young Jewish girl was taken captive in war to a foreign land and enslaved. Her mistress was the wife of Naaman, the second in command of the enemy army. That man, who was greatly responsible for all her woes, contracted leprosy. She then spoke to her mistress about him.

In order to better understand this girl's predicament, keep in mind some of the behind-the-scene activities. After having heard story after story about what has happened in French-speaking West Africa during some of their recent civil wars, we can almost guarantee that the following is well within the possibility of what happened to this young girl. In front of her, Naaman or his men probably commited the following acts:

1. raped her mother
2. killed her father
3. killed her older brothers
4. raped her and took her away to be a slave

Think of all the emotional baggage this young girl carried inside herself. Talk about dysfunctional! Whew, she would be off the chart! Now it might make sense if we were to read that she said to her mistress, "It serves him right." While that would be an understandable response to a series of unfair events, it's not what she said. Instead, she said, "If only my master would see the prophet who is in Samaria! He would cure him of his leprosy" (2 Kings 5:3).

Did we read that correctly? This girl probably went through all of the heartbreak and turmoil listed above, and yet she still knew forgiveness? She still had a heart for God's glory? Yes, that is what the text says. What resulted from her kindness? You know the story. Naaman went to the prophet and got healed. Then he stood before the prophet and said, "Now I know there is no God in all the world except in Israel" (2 Kings 5:16).

This man, a Gentile, the "number two" man in authority in his country's army, stood up and testified about the God of

Israel. Naaman, a Gentile leader, acknowledged God just because a young girl knew forgiveness and had a heart for God's glory! Third, let's move on to the life of Stephen, found in Acts 6–7. You are probably familiar with the story of Stephen. The Bible says Stephen was full of grace and power. It tells us that he did great wonders and performed miraculous signs among the people. But the Sanhedrin opposed him, and they got others to lie about him. He was arrested and taken into court.

As the public heard his testimony, many covered their ears, yelled at the top of their voices, rushed at him, dragged him out of the city, and stoned him. Stephen was stoned to death even though he was full of God's grace and power. (Isn't it interesting that you can be full of the power of God and still be stoned to death?)

The Wrong Question

Now let's review. We've looked at three lives. One was completely blessed (Jabez), one lived through a hell-on-earth experience in order to touch a Gentile's life (the young girl), and one was full of God's power and grace and yet was stoned to death (Stephen)—three totally different lives.

Now here's a simple question for you: Which life was God fair to? The one He completely blessed, the one who had to go through suffering to touch a Gentile, or the one who was stoned to death? While that is a question most people would accept, it's really the wrong question to ask. Life wasn't designed to be fair. Where did we ever get that idea?

Life was designed to be a series of events to reveal God's glory and point us and others to that glory. That is what life is all about! Paul writes, "So whether you eat or drink or whatever you do, do it all for the glory of God" (1 Corinthians 10:31). If that is true, that our purpose is to live for His glory, let's ask a different question: Which of these lives pointed themselves or others to God's glory? The one completely blessed? The young girl who touched a Gentile's life? Or the man full of God's power and grace who was still stoned to death? Naturally the answer is that all three glorified God. One did it by asking God to bless him. God did. And Jabez gave God glory for it. This demonstrated the grace and benevolence of God as a Father. The young Jewish girl knew forgiveness even though she had gone through a hellish life. All of this greatly pointed to God's glory living through her. She was used to influence a Gentile man of great authority and to show God's desire to reach people from all nations. The third one we still talk about today as an example of a man who saw such value in God that he was willing to die for it.

Paul understood this idea. Look again, even more closely, at Romans 11:36, "For from him and through him and to him are *most* things." Is that what it says? No! The Bible doesn't say, "most things;" it says, "all things." "For from him and through him and to him are *all* things." How many is all? Well, it's *all*. *All*—not *some*, a *lot of,* or a *great majority* of. It's *all!*

The trees are to point us to God; the heavens declare His glory; the uniqueness of His botanical creations demonstrate His creativity; the birth of a child is marvelous, and a lion's roar points to God. Car accidents are to point us to God; cancer is to point us to God; heart attacks are to point us to God; an early death is to point us to God. *All* things are to point us and others to Him—not most, a lot of, or even the vast majority of, but *all* things.

R.C. Sproul, in his book *The Invisible Hand,* says it this way: "For the Christian, every tragedy is ultimately a blessing, or God is a liar."[15] That is, everything, not just the good things, is designed to bring us to God. Anything that brings us to our knees is a blessing because life is designed to help us come to a one-on-one encounter with the living God. And if something happens that causes us to get down on our knees, it is ultimately a blessing because it points us to what life is all about—knowing Him, worshiping Him, and praising Him.

There is nothing that can come into a Dog's life that cannot point him or her to God. Hence, life is all about pointing to the glory of God in the midst of blessings *and* in the midst of tough times. It all brings about opportunities to glorify God. That is why Corrie ten Boom could still worship God in a German concentration camp.

A Dog's key verse is found in Habakkuk 3:17–18:

> Though the fig tree does not bud
>> and there are no grapes on the vines,
> though the olive crop fails
>> and the fields produce no food,
> though there are no sheep in the pen
>> and no cattle in the stalls,
> yet I will rejoice in the LORD,
>> I will be joyful in God my Savior.

Cats, on the other hand, only see blessings as being from God, and they expect blessings, to always come out on top, and to always be winners. When the bad things come, they make a cross with their two fingers, as if resisting a vampire, and say, "Get thee behind me, Satan." Dogs know that Christ didn't promise ease and comfort in this life or that Christianity would be easy. Life was designed to be a series of opportunities to live out and radiate the glory of God!

14

Christian Humanism

Eight words literally changed my adult life. I (Bob) remember them clearly. They came at the Black-Eyed Pea restaurant on Alma School Road in Mesa, Arizona, just north of the Superstition Freeway (Route 60). It was just on the right, heading north. We didn't go there often, but we did enjoy it. The memory is vivid in my mind. Debby and I needed a date alone as a couple. Our four young kids were under the age of six, so it was our turn. We had picked up the babysitter and were out for the night. Little did I know what was coming.

I somehow sensed something was wrong. I figured the date would fix it. But no date could ever have fixed this problem. We started talking about trivial things, but there was something missing. We were halfway through dinner when the words came. They were bolts of lightning out of the sky, sending up a warning flare that I needed to heed.

"Honey," Debby finally said, "I need to tell you something."

"What is it?" I said, hoping to myself that it would be something I could fix quickly (like a man from Mars!).

She hesitated, then finally said, "You're no fun to live with anymore."

I was stunned. "Me, no fun?" I thought to myself. I'd never thought of it that way. I was way too busy raising up laborers for the Muslim world to think about having fun. These were eternal destinies I was worrying about—I didn't have time to have *fun*. Little did I know that I was steeped in "evangelical humanism." But before we even look at that, let's talk about humanism as a whole.

Humanism is defined as a system of thought or actions concerned with the interests and ideals of people. Translating that definition into simpler terms, we might assert that humanism proclaims that the reason for all existence is humanity's happiness. It's all about us and making certain we are happy.

Humanism says if you want to take drugs, that's okay as long as you're happy! If you want to sleep around, that's okay too as long as you're happy! And if you want to cheat on your taxes, that's understandable as long as you're happy! Just make sure you are happy. Humanism has so permeated our culture that it has even quietly crept into our Christianity, creating two types of Christian humanism. The first type of Christian humanism is one we call "liberal humanism." The second type is "evangelical humanism." Let's begin by looking at liberal humanism.

Liberal Humanism

Liberal Christian humanism says, The chief end of Christianity is the happiness of people here on earth. This is incorrect. Liberal churches and denominations have embraced liberal humanism. A liberal humanist would say that Christ died to make us happy now, here on earth! The goodness of God is focused on mankind. God made all of creation for us. Jesus died to give us the good life. Angels exist to serve people. I go to church because I've got needs that can be met there. God exists to take care of me and bless me! It's all about me.

A perfect example of this is seen in two of my son's friends who are also brothers. They have a special TV show that they love to watch, but their mom (our close friend as well) is very careful about how much time they spend in front of the television and how much time they spend in God's Word. So she made a deal with her sons. They could watch their half-hour of television if, prior to the show, they had spent half an hour in God's Word.

Well guess what? They started reading their Bibles on a regular basis! Why? They wanted to watch a television show. The emphasis was on what they wanted, not on the fact that God was someone wonderful to spend time with. This motivation and thinking is so typical of Cats. They play the Christian game with God so that they can be blessed! In their hearts, Cats are basically saying, "Lord, I became a Christian because I wanted You to bless me. So bless me, Lord; pour it on!"

If, as Cats think, the purpose of God and all creation is to bless us, and our purpose is to be blessed, how can we best be blessed? The liberal Cat humanist would say, "God wants to bless us with things and good health." Many Cat Christians are certain that is what the Christian life is all about. God blessed Abraham with a long life and things. God blessed Solomon with things when he only asked for wisdom, and He gave him a long life. It must be all about things and a long life.

Admittedly, not many liberal Cat humanists would openly say this, but in private it would seem they believe it and live it. With regard to "things," this is the card of "materialism" that Satan has dealt to them. Their prayer lives are solely focused on asking God for things! As a result, Satan has deceived many into focusing on the good life while missing the holy life. He deludes them into thinking the good life is the same as the Christian life, and the easier, softer, and more comfortable it is, the more spiritual you must be. With regard to a long life, this is the card of "health." Many people believe that if they don't live to the ripe old age of at least seventy, there must be sin in their lives.

Why is Satan happy when Christians seek God for good things and a long life? The focus is no longer on God or His glory. This is why it is wrong. The Cat is basically saying, "Give me what I want, then I'll praise You." While the idea insinuates that God will receive glory, it's contingent upon us getting the stuff we desire. In actuality, Cats live for themselves, not God.

Unfortunately we see this all too often. It manifests itself in the form of "health and wealth theology." And it often encourages Christians to "name it and claim it!" It tells us that God wants us to be rich. It focuses on trusting God to supply all our needs with His riches. These things may not be incorrect, but they are very incomplete in their message. The focus of these messages is not on God. The focus is on people! Is it wrong to be rich in this world? No. But if the riches take you away from focusing on God and His glory, then your priorities are mixed up, your theology is wrong, and God is not pleased. Remember, He is a jealous God.

But it is not only things that Satan gets us to focus on. Along with the wrong priorities, Satan gets liberal humanists to focus on the simple ideal of being happy! There was a young pastor of a struggling church in Pittsburgh, Pennsylvania, whose wife abruptly left him. He went before the elders and asked them what he should do. The elders got together and talked about it. In weighing the pros and cons, they considered how it would affect him to try to save the marriage and how it would affect the church. Should he leave and try to save the marriage or stay and let her go? They concluded that the best thing for him and the church was to let her go so he could stay in Pittsburgh. They did not consider how it would affect God or His reputation. Their shortsighted focus was centered on the happiness of the pastor and the church.

Too many Christians have received advice from one who is reputed to offer "biblical" counseling only to find that advice says, God wants you happy, and since this marriage is tearing you up, go ahead and get a divorce. What does this type of counsel communicate? Life is all about being happy! And if your marriage isn't working out, if you've tried to reconcile and things just aren't getting better, get rid of the marriage. Drop it. You'll be happier divorced. It's all about you.

Evangelical Humanism

Liberal Christianity is not alone in embracing humanism. Evangelical Christianity has been influenced by it too. Satan has a special card for evangelical, spirit-filled Cats. He knows that evangelical Cats don't focus on health and material things as much as others may, so he focuses their attention on the salvation of others. "That's right," he says, "it's not about things; it's about ministering and giving to others, so they can have eternal life too!"

While it is true that one of the ways God chooses to reveal His glory is by having us reach out to others, Satan gets our attention focused on these things to such a degree that saving the lost becomes a greater priority than God and His glory. This is wrong. This unique way of revealing the glory of God can be blown out of proportion so greatly that it can take over the entire Christian life. To keep us motivated and focused in this area, Satan continually reminds us, "Don't forget the lost; it's about the lost. They're going to hell. Focus on the lost."

While liberal Christian humanism says, Christianity is about making people happy while they are on earth, evangelical Christian humanism says, The chief end of Christianity is the happiness of people after they die. In other words, make sure people don't go to hell!

Did you catch the difference? One focuses on people before death, and one focuses on people after death. But both focus on *people*. Why would Satan encourage us to think this way? It replaces God and His glory as the supreme center of our lives! Our attention is on making sure people don't go to hell after they die. So we do everything we can to save people from hell. We motivate people into missions through guilt with comments like, "Thirty-seven thousand Muslims died today and immediately went to hell. What did you do about it?" And all the while, Satan is telling us, "People are going to hell unless you step out to do more, give more, or go to the mission field."

Right now, your mind may be reeling. You may be trying to figure out what could possibly be wrong with keeping people out of hell, and you may be ready to toss this book aside. But stay with us because the truth of this may set you free from guilt.

Is there anything wrong with saving people from hell? Of course not. Then how can it be bad? It is bad in the same way that everything else has been bad. It can replace the priorities of seeing, knowing, and enjoying God's glory and doing everything for His glory. It removes God's glory from its place of primacy and puts people in its place. This can be seen in many areas of the Christian life.

At one large missions conference in England, there were times for the missionaries to share about their ministries. Some had messages of victory; others only gave prayer requests for victory. Each one who spoke about people coming to know Christ (and churches that were started) received a tremendous round of applause. The auditorium erupted with cheers. But missionaries who talked about walking with God, yet who hadn't seen fruit among their target people, received no applause. What was being communicated nonverbally at this missions conference? It's primarily about people coming to know Christ and a little about the glory of the Father.

For those missionaries who had learned the language, persevered in building relationships, stayed on the field in spite of frustration and fatigue, were revealing the glory of God through their patience and pain, and only gave prayer requests—there was no celebration for them. At that meeting, it wasn't about God's glory shining through their perseverance; it was about the lost world and getting them into heaven.

Frontiers, a missions organization, seeks to counter this. They start off their mission statement by saying, "Our passion is to glorify God by planting churches that lead to movements among all Muslim peoples." The first and primary focus is on the glory of God. Then they talk about how they do that through reaching Muslims.

When mankind was first created, Adam and Eve worshiped God. They had one-on-one intimacy with the living God. They sought Him and wanted to walk in the garden with Him in the cool of the day. But when sin entered, Adam and Eve were separated from God. No longer did they desire fellowship with Him; instead, they hid from His presence.

But Jesus' death brought salvation, and while mankind no longer has to die without hope, neither do we have to live without God's fellowship. The cross was designed to not only save us from hell but also bring us back into fellowship with God in order to restore us to that one-on-one intimacy and our worship of Him. Remember, it's about walking toward heaven, not walking away from hell!

But Satan has many people stuck on the theme of saving people from hell. Evangelical Cats can become so focused on saving people from hell that they tend to forget glorifying God through their marriage, their parenting, and their own worship. Evangelism and reaching people has become an end in itself, not a means toward the overall goal of glorifying God. Their focus is on saving people rather than bringing them to the throne of God. Again, Cats have been deceived by Satan.

You can see examples of this on a regular basis. Unfortunately, it is not all that uncommon to hear of wives leaving their husbands while they are in seminary. What is going on there? The husband can become so consumed in preparing to minister to people that he forgets to reveal the glory of God in his marriage. And when he is finally ready to minister, the wife can think, "If this is the way it is going to be our entire married life, I'm out of here."

You can also see this in the lives of some pastors. Their kids are rebellious, their marriages are failing, and their lives are a wreck, but they think that's just the price they have to pay for saving people for Jesus. They are focused on bringing others to Christ but not on showing, displaying, and radiating God's glory in their personal and home lives. Sometimes we're so impressed with their ministries that we excuse everything else. We look at people being won to Christ and think, "How can I challenge that?" Many don't get challenged and end up divorcing years later. But you *can* and should challenge it because our lives are not about people; they are about revealing God's glory in every area of our lives and to all the nations of the earth!

God is glorified when we reach out to people but not when it replaces a glorious, jealous God on His throne. Too many missionaries have come home from the field so consumed with reaching their target people for Christ that they've overlooked godliness in their marriage and parenting. Then once they are home, they end up getting a divorce. Why? They forgot to demonstrate the glory of God in their marriages. They forgot to show the glory of God in their parenting. They were so consumed with reaching others for Christ, that in the process, they dropped other priorities, responsibilities, and obligations that were just as precious.

You see, to some degree, Cats have deified humanity. If we are liberal Christian humanists, we put ourselves on the throne with God and possibly even kick Him off without realizing it. Why? There is not enough room for us, Him, and all those things He blesses us with.

But if we're evangelical humanists, we've put the lost world on the throne. Because it looks so Christian, so spiritual, so good, and it seems to be pleasing to God, we are rarely challenged on it. But the lost world should never replace God on His throne.

With Christian humanism, there is a liberal form and there is an evangelical form. We must guard against living in either extreme, for both have replaced God with people.

The Rescue Mission versus the Treasure Hunt

I (Bob) finally figured out why I rarely share my faith with Americans. (Put me around international people, no problem, but Americans?) I realized that I didn't have "good news" to tell anyone!

Think about it. What was I going to say, "Hey John, do you want to receive Jesus Christ into your life, guaranteeing you eternal salvation? And then you too can have your wife tell you that you're no fun anymore. You too can be worried about one billion Muslims going to hell. You too can burn your candle at both ends trying to 'save' every one of them, and you too can walk around under the weight of the Buddhist, Hindu, and Chinese world, worrying about all those going to hell. Accept this gospel, and you can be a perfect candidate for burnout and have a mild depression for most of the remainder of your life!"

That isn't good news for me or anyone else. That is why my wife sat me down and had a forthright talk with me. The Bible reminded me: "The kingdom of heaven is like treasure hidden in a field. When a man found it, he hid it again, and then in his joy went and sold all he had and bought that field" (Matthew 13:44). I realized that for the majority of my Christian life, I had been on a rescue mission saving Muslims from hell. I hadn't been on a treasure hunt seeking and delighting in the true and living God. And there is a huge difference between the two. Sure I had quiet times. Sure I worshiped the Lord. But it was an occasional glance over my shoulder in the morning, and then for the rest of my day, I was facing hell, seeking to rescue people.

Mark it well. Many evangelicals are on rescue missions, not treasure hunts. The purpose of the ministry of UnveilinGLORY is to prevent people from living that kind of life. Why? We know the danger of a life that has people as its focus and not God. We don't want you to live your life busy on a rescue mission saving people from hell and forgetting the glory of God in other areas. We'd rather your life be seen and understood as one that has found the treasure and points others to the treasure hunt. Those who have found the treasure will naturally want to encourage others to join them. Those who are merely on a rescue mission can lose their families, their ministries, and their very lives while trying to save others.

When Greg Livingstone took over the leadership of a mission agency, he decided to go and visit the missionaries on the field. When he arrived, he figured out why Muslims weren't coming to know Christ. He figured the Muslims were saying, "Hey, you're walking around depressed with tons of guilt on your shoulders. Life looks terrible for you. Whatever it is you've got, I don't want it." Some of those missionaries he encouraged to go home and feel good about themselves.

Contrary to all liberal and evangelical humanism, Dogs say the chief end of Christianity is not to be happy (either before or after death), but rather it is to glorify God. Happiness is not the primary product of the Christian life; it is a byproduct of delighting in God. If you receive the gift of happiness while you glorify God, that's great. But happiness is not the primary goal; it is secondary.

We are here to point to, to radiate, and to reveal His glory in a multitude of ways. When we see God's glory shining through us and realize that it is what life is all about, we can find joy in the fact that we are fulfilling the very purpose for which we were created!

A New Twist

—

Individually and Corporately Glorifying God

When you go into the military, an interesting thing happens. They change you completely. They do this by cutting your hair, giving you a new set of clothes to wear, and breaking you down physically and emotionally, only to build you back up. Within months there's a whole new you!

In a similar sense, this is what we have tried to do to you in this book. We've constantly told you, "It's not about you, it's not about you, it's not about you," hopefully stripping you down emotionally to the point where you are willing to focus on God and His glory. And now that you understand this, we want to tell you something new: it's all about you! What? It's all about us? How can that be?

In the next chapter, we want you to see that the best way you can individually glorify God is by delighting in Him and in Him alone! And in doing that, you'll find your greatest joy. Living passionately for God's glory and seeking your greatest happiness are not mutually exclusive!

In chapter 15, we want you to learn how to see life in a totally different way: as one big worship service for the King. We have taught this material to thousands of believers and are constantly getting reports of changed lives. Our lives too are being changed. As you read this, we hope that you become more like a Dog as well.

In the last chapter, we hope that you'll make the transition from individually glorifying God through your personal delight in Him to corporately bringing Him the greatest glory possible as a part of the human race. The latter is done only one way: by redeeming people from every tongue, tribe, and nation! Global glory will take on a whole new perspective as you begin to fall in love with God in fresh ways and seek to take His glory to the nations! In a nutshell, you'll discover that true Dogs are world Christians!

15

It's All about You!

Her name was Jennifer. She was young, employed, and married to a wonderful man. Like every young bride, she had lots of plans—their own home with a white picket fence, nice cars, and beautiful furniture. It was the great American dream. Life was going her way. But over the span of a few years, Jennifer's life began to change. She and her husband began to drift apart, without even realizing it. And then her greatest fear became a reality: another woman came into the picture. Her husband committed adultery. Jennifer was emotionally crushed and soon divorced. All of her dreams were shattered.

Through all of this, Jennifer began to seek after God. She had to. She had nowhere else to go. She found she had nothing left, and as a result, cried out to God for a relationship with Him. She also began to hunger for God's Word as never before. Throughout the entire ordeal, Jennifer became a strong Christian. Today she is in full-time Christian work, serving on the staff of Frontiers, a mission agency that works to plant churches throughout the Muslim world.

Larry Crabb, in his excellent book *Shattered Dreams*, basically tells us that God is in the business of shattering our dreams.[16] Cats can't understand this because they think, "God doesn't shatter our dreams; He loves us!" But Dogs understand it. Dogs know that God wants to shatter every dream we have that is not of Him. God wants us to have the very best, and the very best happens to be Himself. Anything less than that is settling for second best, and Christ didn't die to give us second best. Therefore, He does (or allows) whatever it takes to get us to give up our inferior dreams and begin to seek Him as our only source of joy. This is what God allowed to happen in Jennifer's life. The great American dream was replaced with an unending hunger for Him!

In *Cat and Dog Theology*, we have been constantly telling you, "It's not about you." What have we meant by that? Simply that it is not about you finding your life's meaning and purpose in things other than God and His glory. Now that you understand this, we want to tell you, "It is about you!" It's about you being your happiest in God and God alone.

No one communicates this better than John Piper. To write a chapter that adequately describes this as well as he does is challenging, especially since his book *Desiring God* communicates it so well.[17] In this chapter, you'll find many of the Scriptures and principles he uses. We encourage you, if you haven't read *Desiring God,* to get it, read it (two, three, and four times), and allow God to use it to change your life!

Nowhere in the Bible does it say that God doesn't want you happy. Cats might think that this is what *Cat and Dog Theology* is trying to say, but it is not. In fact, the Bible (and this book) says just the opposite. Jesus came to give us an abundant life (John 10:10). But this abundant life is not found in things; instead, it is discovered in God Himself! By delighting in Him, we will experience the greatest happiness and joy available in this life. Yes, the Bible does talk about dying to oneself, but this is different from finding your joy in God alone. Look at the texts following.

For whoever wants to save his life will lose it, but whoever loses his life for me *will find it.* (Matthew 16:25, emphasis added)

And everyone who has left houses or brothers or sisters or father or mother or children or fields for my sake *will receive a hundred times as much* and will inherit eternal life. (Matthew 19:29, emphasis added)

Then he said to them all: "If anyone would come after me, he must deny himself and take up his cross daily and follow me. For whoever wants to save his life will lose it, but whoever loses his life for me *will save it.*" (Luke 9:23–24, emphasis added)

If we lose our lives for Christ's sake (for His glory), we find life! In Luke 9:24, the original Greek word is translated "save." When you go to a Greek dictionary, that word is translated "to save, i.e., deliver or protect—heal, preserve, save (self), do well, be (make) whole."[18] When we are saving our lives, we are making them whole, preserving them, and protecting them! It is in sync with Matthew 16:25. We'll "find it!" Life was meant to be found! God is basically saying, "I want you to die to finding your joy in everything *but* Me."

Broken Cisterns

Unfortunately, most Cat Christians are doing the reverse. They are delighting in everything but God and claiming it to be the abundant Christian life. This is what we tried to address in the first two-thirds of this book. God speaks directly to this problem in Jeremiah. Lets look at it together. He says: "My people have committed two sins: They have forsaken me, the spring of living water, and have dug their own cisterns, broken cisterns that cannot hold water" (Jeremiah 2:13).

Here God is using a cistern as a teaching tool. *The American Heritage Dictionary* defines cistern as "a receptacle for holding water or other liquid, especially a tank for catching and storing rainwater." Because water was always a need (and many times a scarcity in Old Testament times), many people would dig holes in the ground to collect rainwater. The holes would fill up during the rainy season, and then the people would use the water for drinking and cooking. The well that Joseph was thrown into was probably a dry cistern (Genesis 37:24). (Note that a cistern is different from a spring. A spring has water continually flowing up into it. Its supply never needs refilling, whereas a cistern constantly has to be filled.)

God tells His people through His prophet Jeremiah that they committed two sins. The first was rejecting the spring of living water—God Himself. This is what Cats have done today. This is what Cat Theology is all about and why this book has been written. They have rejected their first love of Christ and have put themselves or others on the throne. The second sin was that they dug cisterns for themselves, cisterns that leak! Let's look at these leaky cisterns.

What kind of cisterns do Cats dig? Well, the answer to that question is found by asking another question. What delights a Cat? When you find where a Cat finds joy, there you will find a cistern! Cats find their joy outside of God. Though they still go to church and have quiet times, this is not where their joy is. Doing those Christian activities is more of a duty for them than a delight. A Cat's joy comes from other sources. What types of sources?

For men, much joy can come from sports. Whether it is watching their favorite football team, sitting down to watch the World

Series, or going golfing or fishing, most men find more joy in sports than they ever do in the Lord. Is it wrong to get excited about going fishing or watching a game? No. But when you look forward to the next fishing trip or game more than to spending time with God, you've somehow crossed that line. God is not your first love. The sport is. For other men, it can be cars, boats, or homes. The more things they have, the more they feel like "real men," and the more satisfied they are.

For women, it can be clothes or relationships. It can be finding joy in their children or the way their home looks. For young people, it can be sports, movies, the Web, instant messaging, or people of the opposite sex. All of these things can give them more joy than they find in God.

Both men and women can find too much joy in their jobs or careers. Many people pour much of their lives into their careers because that is where their self-image gets the most strokes. (They want those strokes because deep down inside, it's about them.) They spend sixty, seventy, even eighty hours a week at their jobs. To them, that is living!

But God looks at all these activities and declares that those who primarily seek them are digging their own cisterns. They dig them in hopes of finding joy, but they leak. How do they leak?

While at Penn State University, I (Bob) majored in Campus Crusade and minored in my studies. Unfortunately, I learned very few things while there. (But a lot of lives were changed!) One of the few things that I learned was the "IFD disease." The "I" stands for idealization. One of the symptoms is that we envision how much joy it would bring us to have a new car, a new stereo, or a new house. And then once we get it, it's not what we thought it would be. The car was great for the first week, but then it lost its appeal. The stereo was fantastic for the first month, but then we didn't listen to it as much as we thought we would. The home was ideal, but after a few months, it was just like any other home. And after the realization that these things aren't satisfying, we get the "F" part of the disease: frustration. All of a sudden, the empty hole that was there before we had those things is back. And so we go after more toys to fill that hole but find them lacking too. Eventually the "D" sets in: demoralization. We are once again empty, wondering what, if anything, can bring us true, lasting joy.

My (Gerald) mother left me with a tidbit of wisdom and a chuckle to go along with it. She said, "I want what I want when I want it. When I've got what I want, I don't want what I've got, so I didn't really want what I wanted when I wanted it!" Little did she know that she was paraphrasing a portion of Scripture from Proverbs that says, "The eye of man is never full." When God says our cisterns "cannot hold water," this is what He is referring to.

We are going after so many things, yet once we get them, they don't satisfy us. They leak. And as a result, we eventually need the bigger home, the faster car, or the nicer stereo in order to raise our joy level. We are constantly seeking to fill that leaking cistern. We read the Sunday advertisements before we read God's Word. We get more excited about items on sale than meeting with God. And we are so busy seeking after those things that we have little time for God.

God only gets the leftover time. If we have free time, we'll squeeze in a quiet time. But meeting with God (and therefore learning to delight in Him) is always the second priority. (It amazes me how some people can spend six hours on the golf course on a Saturday but not find time to adequately meet with God.)

Unfortunately, before the frustration sets in, a Cat feels satisfied (they think they've got the abundant Christian life). And at that point, a Cat's Christian life is similar to eating out at some Mexican restaurants. How is that? You sit down, you order your food, and out come salsa and chips. So, you stuff yourself for a while with chips and salsa, and when the main meal comes, quite honestly, you're not hungry!

This is how Cats are. "A two-hour quiet time?" a Cat cries out. "Isn't that rather extravagant? Isn't meeting with God for ten minutes every other day enough? An all-night prayer meeting? What have you got to pray about that takes all night? You can't want that many things; that's selfish!"

God doesn't want this for our lives. This is why He says:"Whoever finds his life will lose it, and whoever loses his life for my sake will find it" (Matthew 10:39). God knows that the things of this world can't truly satisfy us. This is why He said that we need to die to ourselves. He doesn't want us to seek one dream after another and get frustrated and demoralized in the process. That isn't the abundant life He wants for us.

Spring of Living Water

Contrary to the broken cistern, God says He is like the spring of living water. The beauty of the spring is that you never have to refill it. It has a constant supply of water for those who want to drink! Remember, God is infinite. And if He's infinite, there is an infinite amount of Him that we can get to know and enjoy. We will never get to the point of spending time with God and say, "Okay, I've been there and done that; this is old."

In John 4, Jesus talked to the woman at the well about living water. She asked Him what He was talking about. Listen to His answer: "Jesus answered, 'Everyone who drinks this water will be thirsty again, but whoever drinks the water I give him *will never thirst*. Indeed, the water I give him will become in him a *spring of water* welling up to eternal life'" (John 4:13–14, emphasis added).

God wants us never to be thirsty again. He wants us so satisfied in Him and Him alone that we will not go after the things of the world to find happiness. We will not search for sexual relationships outside of marriage; we will not covet things to satisfy us. We will be so content to see God and His glory that life will

CAT AND DOG THEOLOGY

be abundant in the truest sense. We will want to reflect Him and His glory everywhere because we will be so satisfied in Him! And the more we are satisfied in Him alone, the more we reflect His value and the more glory goes to Him! The motto of John Piper's ministry, Desiring God Ministries, is "God is most glorified in us when we are most satisfied in Him."

Although Cats would say they want to be satisfied in God, Cats don't have the patience for it. Cats always want a quick fix, and the things of this world can give it to them. Those quick fixes are all around them, from next weekend's football game to the new movie coming out at the theater to the mall down the road. But finding the spring of living water takes time. There are no quick fixes with God.

Look at Proverbs 2:1–5:

> My son, *if* you accept my words
> and store up my commands within you,
> turning your ear to wisdom
> and applying your heart to understanding,
> and *if* you call out for insight
> and cry aloud for understanding,
> and *if* you look for it as for silver
> and search for it as for hidden treasure,
> *then* you will understand the fear of the LORD
> and find the knowledge of God. (emphasis added)

Did you notice the "if / then" clause? The "if" part is challenging. If we store up His commands within us (memorizing Scripture and meditating), if we turn our ears to wisdom and apply our hearts to understanding (sitting under biblical teaching on a steady basis), if we call out for insight and cry aloud for understanding (making our schedules revolve around our quiet times, not the other way around), if we search for God's Word like a hidden treasure (note how different that is from giving God our leftover time), *then* we will find God. Dogs understand that seeking the spring of living water takes time and won't bring instant results. They know that FedEx (when it absolutely has to be there overnight) is rare when seeking God.

> I *wait* for the LORD, my *soul waits*,
> and in his word I put my hope.
>
> *My soul waits for the Lord*
> more than watchmen wait for the morning,
> more than watchmen wait for the morning."
> (Psalms 130:5–6, emphasis added)
>
> *Wait for the LORD*;
> be strong and take heart
> and *wait for the LORD*." (Psalm 27:14, emphasis added)
>
> I *waited patiently* for the LORD." (Psalm 40:1, emphasis added)
>
> Yes, LORD, walking in the way of your laws,
> *we wait for you*;
> your name and renown
> are the desire of our hearts." (Isaiah 26:8, emphasis added)

We should seek God like pirates seeking for hidden treasure. It doesn't happen in a day. Sometimes it can take an entire lifetime. Waiting for the Lord is what Dogs are comfortable doing. (Cats hate to wait.) This is why Dogs expect UPS—an Unrelenting, Patient Search. They know that "soul waiting" exposes their soul to God. It helps them (and God) show how much they truly hunger after God. Soul waiting also shows the value of God to you. If you wait for something for years, it must be very valuable to you. But if you give up after a few minutes, it isn't very valuable. (Because Cats don't want to wait on God, they are nonverbally communicating, "God, You're not worth waiting for.") This is why the Scriptures command us to delight in God!

> Rejoice in the Lord always. I will say it again: Rejoice! (Philippians 4:4)

> Finally, my brothers, rejoice in the Lord! (Philippians 3:1)

> But may all who seek you rejoice and be glad in you. (Psalm 40:16)

> One thing I ask of the LORD,
>   this is what I seek:
> that I may dwell in the house of the LORD
>   all the days of my life,
> to gaze upon the beauty of the LORD
>   and to seek him in his temple. (Psalm 27:4)

"But just how exactly do you rejoice in the Lord?" cries a Cat. In his book *A Hunger For God,* John Piper basically says, "Fast from whatever pleases you more than God."[19] For some that may mean fasting from shopping; for some it may mean fasting from television; for others it may mean fasting from the Internet.

Whatever keeps you so content that you don't want God, fast from it! We agree with him wholeheartedly. But we hope to answer that Cat's question more in the next chapter.

16

Worship Is Life!

Orel Herschiser was a pitcher for the Los Angeles Dodgers. In 1988, he had an incredible season. He pitched a shutout game in August followed by five more shutouts in the regular season, as well as multiple shutout innings. He kept his opponents from scoring an earned run in fifty-nine consecutive innings.

In the National League playoffs against the New York Mets, Orel continued to dominate hitters, pitching more than twenty-four innings and another complete game shutout in the final game! In the World Series against the Oakland A's, Orel had another complete game victory in game five that clinched the Series for the Dodgers. At the end of the season, Orel was awarded the Cy Young award and two MVP awards, one for the National League playoffs and the other for the World Series.

During one of the playoff games, the TV cameras zoomed in on Orel in the dugout between innings. They could tell he was singing softly to himself but couldn't decipher the song. The announcers wondered what he was singing and commented that Orel's record certainly gave him something to sing about.

When Orel was on "The Tonight Show" a few days later, the host asked him to sing the song he had been caught singing on tape. The audience roared its approval at this suggestion. So on national TV, Orel softly sang these words:

> Praise God, from whom all blessings flow;
>> Praise Him, all creatures here below;
>> Praise Him above, ye heav'nly host;
>> Praise Father, Son, and Holy Ghost. Amen.

In the midst of a baseball game, Orel had been singing praises to God.[20]

At the end of chapter 1, we looked at Revelation 4:11 and translated it to say: "You are worthy, our Lord and God, to receive glory and honor and power, for You created all things, and *for your pleasure* they were created and have their being."

God created everything for His own pleasure. That means all of the stars are here for God's pleasure. This earth is here for God's pleasure, along with the sun and the moon. The trees and flora are here for God's pleasure. The birds and insects are here for God's pleasure. Anything and everything you can think of is here for God's pleasure.

Cats want to know how that "anything" relates to them (because life is all about them). They are constantly asking the question, "What do I get out of that?" Dogs ask a different question because they know everything is here for Him. Hence they ask, "What does God get?" (WDGG?) Because of this, Dogs are constantly holding worship services throughout their days, because in everything they do, they are relating to God. This is not the way it is with Cats.

Cat Worship

Make no mistake about it, Cats worship. But it is merely a *part* of their lives. Cats worship only during specific times. These times occur on Sunday mornings at church, during their personal quiet times, or when they are listening to worship music. And what do they worship God for? Their worship is primarily focused on thanking Him for what He's done for *them*. (Remember, it's all about them. It's like a cancer; they've got it and don't even realize it.) Their favorite songs have a lot of *me's*, *my's*, and *I's* in them. And when they aren't worshiping God for what He's done for them, everything else is just "regular life."

Dogs worship God too. But when they worship on Sunday mornings or during their personal quiet times, they primarily focus on who He is, not so much what He's done for them. Songs like "How Great Thou Art" and "Holy, Holy, Holy" are very familiar to them not because they're catchy tunes that make them happy, but because they rightfully exalt God for who He is! And when they're finished with their worship service, their worship doesn't stop. Dogs don't know a "regular life" outside of God's glory. To a Dog, worship is life itself!

When I (Bob) got married, someone encouraged me to get a hobby so I could take my mind off work. As a result, I took up woodworking. I bought some old tools and began to build. My first project was a small tray for my new bride. We still use it. I eventually progressed to the point where I took on a huge project. I decided I was going to build my own roll-top desk. For various reasons, I used no plans, and I would only use scrap lumber I gathered on the burn piles of the condominiums going up around us. Today it sits in our home.

When people walk in and see that desk, they say to my wife, "Wow, that's a beautiful desk. Where did you get that?" My wife responds with the truth, "My husband made that desk from scratch." When I hear the word "scratch," I follow my cue and (try to) humbly walk in at that time. And when I get there, they say, "You made that from scratch?" At that point in time, they are honoring me for the work of my hands. When I realized what was going on, a light went off in my head. "Why can't I honor God for the work of His hands?"

Since I have begun to think that way, I have discovered a multitude of ways for life to be a worship service. One time I was driving my car down the 605 highway on my way to San Diego with my daughter, Elise (my kids get one trip a year with Dad). On the side of the road, we noticed beautiful flowers. So we stopped, got out, and picked one.

As we made our way back to the car, we began to study the details of the flower. I said, "Look, Sis. Look at those colors. Look at the purples and the greens—at how beautiful it is. And would you have ever thought to put these two colors together? This didn't happen by accident you know; God painted this. God is a masterful artist. And look at the leaves. Look how green they are. Look at the veins. Feel the tiny hairs on the stem. And smell it, Sis. Doesn't it smell wonderful?"

What was happening? For ten minutes on the side of the 605 highway, my daughter and I held a worship service because we were asking one question: What does God get out of this?

But I wasn't always that way. When I was steeped in my evangelical-humanism days, I vividly remember someone giving me a rose and telling me how beautiful it was. When I got that rose, I took one look at it and threw it over my shoulder to the ground. Why? It didn't have anything to do with reaching Muslims for Christ. I literally didn't have any time for smelling the roses!

And aquariums? I hated aquariums. I would look at one fish, go to the next tank, then to the next, and work my way through it as fast as I could, always aware of where the exit was. Oh how I was bored with aquariums! But now, I can't get out of them! I love aquariums! I love them because I look at God's creativity and I am awed! I imagine God thinking through the different fish he made, from the swordfish to the sunfish, some with ugly faces and others with plain faces. And then I'm amazed at His creativity with the octopus and the way it can change its color to match its environment.

I also love His colorful designs on the fish. I delight in the stripes and the way He gently blends His colors. He is the master painter. I laugh at the sea horse. I'm staggered by the whale. The crabs can make me smile. And the beauty of a jellyfish swimming—no art mankind has ever made has come close to that! It used to be that time in the aquarium dragged; now it flies. I can't get out of aquariums because I am overcome by His creativity, and I keep thinking about the joy our Father must have had during Genesis 1:20–21.

As I sit here at my son's flag-football practice, writing on my laptop, I'm watching a beautiful sunset. God's gentle blending of the pinks and grays are amazing! His design in the cloud patterns is so creative. I am thanking Him and praising Him for the sunset. I am holding a mini-worship service watching a sunset at my son's flag-football practice. (We constantly try to teach this to our kids by getting them to say, "Look what God is painting in the sky!")

Sharon and I (Gerald) enjoy sharing life experiences with each other as well. While driving in the car, if I see a gorgeous sunset, I'll pick up my cell phone and call her and encourage her to look at it. Since we've been impacted with God's glory, our conversations have taken quite a turn. I used to say, "Look at the beautiful sunset!" But now she hears, "Look at the beautiful sunset; God sure does good work!" The more you begin to focus on God and His glory in the work of His hands, the more life comes alive—conversations change and your appreciation of God's handiwork grows. But those are not the only things we see. There's another dimension!

When we (Bob and Debby) lived in Arizona, we owned a house that had a door to the garage that was very difficult to close. You really had to slam it shut, and with four small children, it was rarely closed. Usually the air conditioning escaped. The day finally came when I found the time to fix it. After getting the proper screws, I put them through the hinges and drilled them in, hoping to catch at least two, if not three, studs. Finally after all nine were drilled, I held my breath and closed the door. To my joy (things don't usually work out the way they're supposed to on the first try—Murphy's Law always follows me), the door closed without even the slightest hesitation! It was fixed.

I know this sounds dumb, but I would go out there at certain times and open the door just so I could close it! I got so much joy out of having the door work right! Then it hit me again. If I'm getting so much joy out of having something work right, I bet God is also getting joy out of having things work right! And if He is getting joy out of it, why can't I?

When God first changed my (Gerald's) focus toward His glory, even my prayer life drastically changed. My wife would probably rather I not tell this story, but it is important to me. We had a dog named Punkie. While taking her for a walk so she could do her "business," I noticed that she was having difficulty. She would squat and nothing would happen. She walked a little farther and nothing happened. She tried to walk while still squatting, and nothing happened. So I prayed that God would heal my dog.

I was struck with the realization that nothing in my prayer acknowledged God, His handiwork, His creation, or His glory. I knew I had to pray again but differently this time. Now I prayed, "Lord, you blessed us with this little dog, and what a joy she has been. But, Lord, she's having trouble now. This little body You created with such splendor and so many little organs and tissue that work to show off Your glory, Lord, is not showing it off right now. I'm asking You to make these parts that You designed work the way You intended. Show off what You made, and allow it to work right!"

I shouldn't have been amazed, but Punkie squatted and did her thing at that very moment. Okay, so it's a little crude, and it's a story I don't share from every pulpit, but it certainly shows how God's glory can be seen in any of life's experiences!

Delight in What God Delights In

So now when we (Debby and Bob) see a couple holding hands on a walk with their children, we know that God is up in heaven smiling because the family unit is working the way it was designed to work. And if God is smiling, we can smile too! When we see a mother or father loving a child with kisses and hugs, we feel joy because we know God is joyful. And this has changed our lives!

We used to hold our children in our arms and think about the next meeting, tomorrow's plans, or the lost Muslim world, and we never really enjoyed our kids. Now when we hold them, we are worshiping God by thanking Him for a father-son relationship or a mother-daughter relationship. We are awed by the idea that He entrusted us to love these children and train them in His ways. We delight in spending time with them (even though it is never enough!), in watching them practice football or dance in ballet and tap, and in seeing them grow and develop. And now we know why God gave us grandchildren: to have a second chance.

When a husband dates his bride of fifteen years, God smiles. So can we. When a young man dates a young girl and treats her with holiness and respect, God smiles. So can we. When the seasons change like clockwork, God smiles. And we can enjoy them too. When two people reconcile and forgive each other, God is smiling. And if we learn about it, we too can share that joy. Whatever is working right, the way God designed it to work, gives God pleasure. Everything was created for His pleasure (Revelation 4:11). If you know that He is smiling about something, then smile with Him. It's not about you; it's about Him! Christian Dogs celebrate with God in the joy He has!

Do we need more examples? Listening to music can be one big worship service. This is not because of the beat or the tune, although that may add to it. But the whole idea of a piece of metal pulled tightly across some wood and then rubbed by horse's hair so that it vibrates air molecules that go into the wood and eventually reach some skin in my ear which vibrates a drum that sends a signal to my brain, and I interpret that as music—what a miracle! What a God! And it's not just one pitch; I can hear thousands of different tones. Some blend together nicely. Some contrast with each other. And somehow I know which ones sound nice and which are off. It's amazing! I am in awe of the God who created sound!

And then think of sight. Sure, the eighth grade taught us all about rods and cones. But somehow deep down inside, I thought that the signals sent from those rods and cones were sent into the brain, played on a projector, and someone was inside the brain watching it. No. Somehow the gray matter determines an object as an image that makes sense. Unbelievable! Dogs come to the realization that just to be able to see is worthy of worship! What an awesome God we have!

Fall is a wonderful time—watching the Lord paint leaves that were once green with life. I love how He can take a green tree and paint only a corner of the leaves bright orange or yellow! My fall drives take me down the road, glimpsing tree after tree and declaring, "Lord, how creative You are!" A big smile comes across my face.

The next time you get bored, take a nature walk around your house. Look at a bush. Are some parts of it thriving with life while others are dead? Study it. Think about it. Learn from it. The Lord designed it that way. What does it tell you? I've done this and found that God is quite happy with life and death together. Both life and death are the same to God.

Gary Taylor helped start Frontiers, a missions agency which plants churches throughout the Muslim world. Over time, the Lord called us in separate directions, but I (Bob) always kept in touch with him. Once when we were both at an international council of Frontiers to honor Greg and Sally Livingstone, Gary and his wife Carolyn shared about their son's battle with cancer. One of the stories that I have never forgotten was Carolyn's portrayal of their son, Derek, lying in a hospital bed battling cancer, close to death, and holding his newborn nephew. Life and death together—something the Lord is not afraid to position together. I've seen it on bushes and trees, and now I was hearing about it in my friend's son. Oh what a picture of the glory of the Lord!

If you're easily bored with nature walks, go to your kitchen and pull out an orange, a grape, a watermelon, or a cupcake and taste it! Have you stopped to realize that God didn't have to give you taste buds? But He did so you could taste His glory! You see, God could have made everything taste the same, like chicken. He could have made it all bland and tasteless, like water. But He didn't. He wanted you to taste a chocolate-covered strawberry, barbecue, peach nectar, butter pecan, and more. Each taste should bring an exclamation of admiration of His handiwork. Maybe instead of just thanking God for your provision of food, you should stop in the middle of a meal you are enjoying and tell God how great He is for allowing you to have the sensation of taste.

God's glory is all around us. It can be seen in so many ways. Never stop looking for it. Never stop hungering for it. Never stop being awed by it! Radiate to God the glory He is worthy of! Life should be one big worship service. And depending on whether you are a Dog or a Cat, everything will take on a different meaning.

So what do Dogs actually do differently when life is one big worship service? The answer may shock you: not much. But whatever they do, they do it with a whole new attitude! They wash dishes thinking, "This is pleasing to God." They work thinking, "This is the role that God has given me as the caretaker for this family." They change diapers thinking, "I'm taking care of the ones that God has entrusted to me, and I know this pleases God." They drive to work wondering, "How can I reflect God's glory in how I drive, and in how I see His glory in the sights around me?" They watch a child at the airport holding a parent's hand and inwardly yell, "Yes, that's the way God designed it to be!" They fix a wonderful dinner for their family saying, "This is the role the Lord has me in, and it is reflecting His glory. I am at peace with it and satisfied with it!"

Dogs do everything that Cats do. Their lives are parallel in every way except one: their mindset! They do everything as an act of worship to God and to make Him smile. This is because they define everything in terms of God's glory! (See A Dog's Glossary of Terms.)

Life was designed to be one big worship service as we live for and reflect the glory of the Lord. But with Cat Theology, we have turned it around so that we no longer worship the Lord. We've been busy worshiping ourselves. Oh how we need to dive into Dog Theology and once again worship the Lord for who He is and not for what He can give to us. Tommy Tenney aptly describes a Cat's focus when he asks whether we are looking for God's hand (to see what He will give us) or God's face (to delight in being in His presence).

It is our hope and prayer that your life will be radically changed by the contents of this book. And maybe you'll have good news to tell others for the very first time! Oh Father, please make it happen. Amen.

17

God's Greatest Glory!

When I (Gerald) was serving as a pastor in the Netherlands, a few of the folks in our church were devoted admirers of Corrie ten Boom, a Dutch woman who was imprisoned by the Germans during World War II for hiding Jews. These church members served as volunteer guides in Corrie's old home, which guests can still visit today and hear her tale of survival, hope, and faith. Corrie's story has been retold on film and in print as *The Hiding Place*, and Corrie has shared her story and testimony around the world through her own ministry and as a guest of Billy Graham.[21]

The story began when someone informed the Nazis that Corrie's strong Christian family were hiding Jews in their home. They were discovered, and Corrie and her family were sent to a concentration camp. Corrie lost her entire family but not her faith. She lived on and told others about the God who not only allowed her to survive but also empowered her to forgive those who persecuted and tormented her.

Long after the war, Floyd McClung of YWAM visited Corrie ten Boom (who was seventy years old). He noticed she had just purchased new luggage. Floyd, very surprised to see a lady of Corrie's age buying luggage, asked her why she had made this purchase. Corrie told him that an angel had visited her in a vision. When he inquired as to why the angel had come, she told him that God had sent the angel to let her know that she had ten more years to live. So Corrie went out and celebrated by purchasing brand new luggage.

Five years later, Corrie's health diminished to the point that she suffered greatly and had very limited mobility. While in the hospital in terrible pain, Floyd came to visit again. In their conversation, he was told that a second angel had visited her. This angel had informed her that the pain and agony she was going through was going to result in her death, and that she was never going to get better. Corrie had protested, telling the angel that she had five more years to live. The angel responded by saying that her heavenly Father was aware of this but had sent the angel to tell her that He was willing to take her home early. With that, Corrie was faced with a troubling decision: go on to be with the Lord or endure incredible suffering and pain for another five years?

How would you reply? Maybe the same way we would. We would choose to avoid the pain, escape the hardship, and eliminate the suffering. Why would anyone choose anything different? It's at times like this when we discover what people are made of. And we learn what made Corrie ten Boom different.

Corrie answered the angel with a question, "Which will bring my Father the greatest glory? Going to be with Him now or enduring the five years of suffering?" The angel said, "Staying here and enduring five more years." And with that, Corrie gave her answer, "Then that is what I choose."

How could she have made such a decision? What made her so different? Simply this: Corrie didn't live for her own ease and comfort; she lived for the glory of her Father.

What came of those five years? While Corrie ten Boom had been a household name among millions of Christians around the world before that time, God used those last years to seal in the hearts and minds of many more people a picture of what it means to live faithfully. Corrie has shown that life is to be lived for our Father's glory and not for ourselves—even if it means enduring pain and suffering.

This causes us to ask a very simple question, How much glory do we want to give to God? Do we want to give him some glory, a lot of glory, or maximum glory? We will assume that since you've made it this far in the book, you are committed to bringing your heavenly Father maximum glory. How do we do that? The answer is found in world evangelization when we ask, "What does God get out of it" rather than, "What do people get out of it?"

Global Glory

In order to understand what God gets out of world evange-lization, we need to look at another question and that is, What happens to our vision of God when we worship God with people from other cultures? Have you ever experienced worshiping God with someone from another culture? In our seminars, we ask for a show of hands of how many people have done this. We usually get quite a few. And we ask those who raise their hands, "What did it do to your vision of God?"

We always get the same answer. "It got bigger," they say in various forms, meaning God got more glory when they worshiped Him with people from other cultures. There is a principle hidden in those answers and that principle is: God gets more glory when He unifies that which is diverse.

In other words, take two diverse things and unite them in the name of Jesus Christ, and God gets more glory. Whether it is a couple on the verge of divorce, and you heal their marriage through the Scriptures or it is a Palestinian and an Israeli, and you create a God-honoring relationship after centuries of bitter animosity, God gets greater glory. Add to those four a Kuwaiti and an Iraqi who set aside their bitterness and hatred in the name of Jesus, and God gets more glory. Throw in an Aceh from Indonesia and a Karalkolpoch from Uzbekistan, and God gets even more glory because when more diversity is united, more glory is given.

This is why God has communicated clearly in His Word that He wants people from *every* tongue, tribe, people, and nation (Revelation 5:9). You know He didn't have to do it that way. He could have said, "I want you to reach 10 percent of the world" (which is roughly what we are doing now), or, "Go make disciples of 70 percent of the world." God could have put a percentage on it, but He didn't. He was very specific about people from *every* tongue, tribe, people, and nation. Why?

The answer is simple. It deals with the fact that He is a jealous God. You see, if God had only reached the Jews, He would have received glory, but not the maximum glory. If He had reached the Jews and a lot of Gentile groups, He would have received even more glory, but not the greatest glory. Only when you and I are there with people from every tongue, tribe, and nation (meaning all our diversities are united), then our Father will get the greatest glory He could ever have from mankind. The true driving force for world evangelization is to bring our Father the greatest glory possible.

And the seed of this is found in the very first command to all of mankind. It is found in Genesis 1:28: "God blessed them and said to them, 'Be fruitful and increase in number; fill the earth and subdue it.'" Did you catch those words "fill the earth"? Do you know what happens over centuries of time (God is in no rush) when you "fill the earth"? Your language begins to break apart, and over time you move from a slight accent to a totally different language, creating diversity!

We believe this is the heart of the very first command to mankind. God intended to create diversity so later He could bring it together in harmony to reveal His greatest glory! This is why true Dogs are "world Christians," believers who seek to reach all nations and ethnic groups for the greatest glory of their Father. And this shifts their motivation in everything.

No longer is missions a duty where someone says, "Well, someone has to go. I guess I will since no one else is volunteering." No longer is missions purposed on just getting people into heaven. Now there is a higher and greater motivation: "I want to go to the nations because I want to see my Father glorified among all people groups of the world for His greatest glory!" This gives us a fresh new motivation for doing missions. Yes, people are lost and going to hell, but God's greatest glory will be revealed when we reach every one of them. Therefore, let's reach the world to reveal our Father's greatest glory!

No longer is missions imprecise for the missions committee, sending people with no knowledge of what people group they are going to or whether they are reached or unreached. "So you're going to India, huh? Okay, we'll support you with fifty dollars a month." Now missions is very specific with committees asking key questions such as, "Which people group are you going to? Are they a reached or unreached people group?" They know that by prioritizing the unreached people groups, we will be moving more quickly toward the goal of bringing our Father His greatest glory!

This complements what John Piper says in the opening paragraph of his book *Let the Nations Be Glad.*

> Missions is not the ultimate goal of the church. Worship is. Missions exists because worship doesn't. Worship is ultimate, not missions, because God is ultimate, not man. When this age is over and the countless millions of the redeemed

fall on their faces before the throne of God, missions will be no more. It is a temporary necessity. But worship abides forever.[22]

The Story of the Bible

The goal of bringing every ethnic group before the living God to reveal His greatest glory is the story of the Bible. Too many people read their Bibles with a limited view. They study it as sixty-six independent books with various lessons and themes interwoven throughout. But the Bible was meant to be read as one book. And just as every book has an introduction, a story, and a conclusion, the Bible also has an introduction, a story, and a conclusion.

The introduction is found in Genesis 1–11, the story starts in Genesis 12 and runs through to Revelation 3, and the conclusion begins in Revelation 4. The introduction is simple. You know most of it. God creates everything and says it is good. Adam and Eve fall into sin. God takes care of the sin problem. People begin to multiply, but so does the sin. Every intention of their hearts is evil. God, being a holy God, cannot tolerate all of the sin. So God brings about a judgment by sending a flood.

Noah and his family get into an ark and float through a huge storm for forty days and nights. After a year, the flood subsides. God gives Noah a rainbow and says to him, "I am never going to flood the earth again." Humanity begins to grow and multiply again. And then we get to Genesis 11:1. This verse is key in understanding the introduction to the story of the Bible: "Now the whole world had one language and a common speech."

Notice the idea behind this. There was no diversity, no "us versus them" mentality. There was only an "us." They were one people with one language and one culture. There was no possibility of bringing God His greatest glory because there were no differing people groups. Notice what happens next in verses 3–4. Instead of obeying God and spreading out as they were commanded to do (creating diversity), they disobey and remain one people.

> They said to each other, "Come, let's make bricks and bake them thoroughly." They used brick instead of stone, and tar for mortar. Then they said, "Come, let us build ourselves a city, with a tower that reaches to the heavens, so that we may make a name for ourselves and not be scattered over the face of the whole earth." (Genesis 11:3–4)

For whatever reason (one can only guess), they refused to obey God and sought to remain one people, directly disobeying God.

Jealous (a name for God found in Exodus 34:14) wasn't worried. He was committed to seeing His glory revealed in such a way that would create diversity and later allow Him to unite it in harmony. So He did in one moment what should have taken centuries to do. He took their common language and broke it down into many different languages, instantly creating diversity. In this way He could make them spread out and then bring them back together in harmony at some later date. Now, instead of just one group of people, there were many groups of people. And the stage was set for God to work His "greatest glory" campaign!

This ends the introduction of the story of the Bible. If we were watching this in a theater, the curtains would close for a short intermission. We would go out and get a drink and some popcorn, and then we'd come back in to see the beginning of the story of the Bible. We would be curious about how God might fulfill His desire for fellowship with mankind, especially since it is now divided into so many groups. How He will do it will be the key factor in the story that is to come. As the curtain opens, the

stage would be set with God in the heavens looking down on all
of the people groups He had created but who were all separated
from Him. He would then reach down and pick up one of them
(Abraham) and make a promise to him. The promise would have
two parts. First, He would say to Abraham, "I want to bless you."
Second, He would say, "I want you to be a blessing to all of the
families on the face of the earth."

This is called the Abrahamic Covenant or the Abrahamic
Promise. It is found in Genesis 12 and reads like this:

> I will make you into a great nation
>   and I will bless you;
> I will make your name great,
>   and you will be a blessing.
> I will bless those who bless you,
>   and whoever curses you I will curse;
> and all peoples on earth
>   will be blessed through you." (Genesis 12:2–3)

As God spoke of blessing others through Abraham, He used a
simple word, which has tremendous impact on His glory. He used
the word "all." "All peoples on earth will be blessed through you."
Not "some," "most," or even "a large number of," but "all peoples
on earth will be blessed through you."

Put into New Testament language, God is basically giving the
Great Commission. "Go therefore and make disciples of all nations" (Matthew 28:19) and "All peoples on earth will be blessed
through you" (Genesis 12:3) basically say the same thing. God
told Abraham that through Him all people on earth would be
blessed, and through Jesus He told the disciples that all nations
would be reached.

These two passages are parallel, and Dogs know why. God has
been, is, and always will be going after the revelation of His greatest

glory, and that will only come when all people groups have representatives coming together to celebrate God. He knew that from the very beginning. To emphasize this, immediately after God created the nations, He made the promise to Abraham to reach every one of them. He was making it perfectly clear. He is seeking to redeem people from every tongue, tribe, and nation! God's desire to reach all nations permeates both the Old and the New Testaments. Let's look at a few examples from the Old Testament:

> "Be still, and know that I am God; I will be exalted *among the nations*, I will be exalted in the earth." (Psalm 46:10, emphasis added)

> Sing to the LORD, *all the earth*;
>   proclaim his salvation day after day.
> Declare his glory *among the nations*,
>   his marvelous deeds *among all peoples*.
> (1 Chronicles 16:23–24, emphasis added)

> For as the soil makes the sprout come up,
>   and as a garden causes seeds to grow,
>   so the Sovereign LORD will make righteousness
> and praise spring up before *all nations*. (Isaiah 61:11, emphasis added)

And from the New Testament:

> He told them, "This is what is written: The Christ will suffer and rise from the dead on the third day, and repentance and forgiveness of sins will be preached in his name *to all nations,* beginning at Jerusalem." (Luke 24:46–47, emphasis added)

> Therefore go and make disciples of *all nations.*
> (Matthew 28:19, emphasis added)

The Conclusion

Does God pull off what He set out to do at the beginning? Does He get His greatest glory? How does it end? Let's quickly look in the back of our Bibles and see how the story concludes. In Revelation 5:9, we have a song being sung by the elders and living creatures. This has got to be a very important song. Can you imagine the elders of your church getting up in front of your congregation to sing a song? And if it is so important, we'd better pay close attention to it. What does it say? It says:

And they sang a new song:
> You are worthy to take the scroll
> and to open its seals,
> because you were slain,
> and with your blood you purchased men for God
> from every tribe and language and people and nation.
> (Revelation 5:9)

Notice where they came from: "every tribe and language and people and nation!" What God set out to do through Abraham, God pulls off at the very end of time! And because untimate diversity is represented through all nations, God receives ultimate glory! God has declared that this will happen. He has decreed it. He has demanded it. Why? He desires it.

If you were to take your Bible and put your thumb on Genesis 12 and your other fingers at Revelation 5:9, you would have a story in between—a story of a loving God seeking to redeem people from every ethnic group on the face of the earth. Most Cats are blind to this. Most Dogs know it well. That's why

Dogs are world Christians, passionately pursuing the nations for their Father's greatest glory. It's the story of the Bible! In fact, if you were to take missions out of the Bible, you'd have very little left to study—just a few chapters in Genesis and a few in Revelation. (To learn more about the story of the Bible, please read *Unveiled At Last* by Bob Sjogren.)

We hope that whatever happens in your life, you, like Corrie ten Boom, will seek to ask your heavenly Father, "What will bring You the most glory?" And you'll pursue His glory in every area of life and somehow play a role in taking that glory to the ends of the earth! Instead of living from birth to death seeking that which is safe, soft, and comfortable, you will live with a purpose: the purpose of glorifying God!

If you're going to be a dog, be a pointer—always pointing to His glory.

Epilogue

We have found that many Christians, pastors, and churches have over-reacted to our message of Dog Theology. They have left our seminars and the reading of this book determined to develop a "Dog Theology Life-Style" or a "Dog Theology Church" only to find themselves out of balance—and very unattractive to others. Then, as the numbers in their churches diminish they rationalize it by saying those who left were just not "spiritual."

That raises an important question: "Is Dog Theology unbalanced?" The way to bring an uneven seesaw into balance is not to sit in the middle but to go to the other end. With centuries of Cat Theology at one end of the seesaw, it has been our strategy through our book and in our seminars to over-emphasize the "glory of God" aspect in our description of Dog Theology. But this is only to counter-balance the decades and centuries of Cat Theology that has permeated our churches. The practice of *real* Dog Theology is a matter of proper balance and priorities.

Year upon year, decade upon decade, and century upon century of Cat Theology needs to be brought into balance by a predominant weight of Dog-thinking. But this heavy emphasis is in this book and in our seminars only to adjust our thinking. Living it out is another matter and requires a different strategy.

That raises the question, What is a proper balance? Or better yet, What is pure Dog Theology? To answer this question we need to remember a few primary points:

1. Cat Theology is not incorrect—it is just incomplete;
2. Dog Theology is not the absence of Cat Theology—it is the completion of it;
3. Christ died both for us and the glory of God.

Now imagine a train barreling down the tracks. The train runs on two tracks, and if at any point we eliminate either rail, the train will not arrive at its destination—it will derail.

Let's label one rail *Us* and the other rail *Glory of God*. Cat Theology focuses on only one rail—it is all about *Us*. You may have thought that Dog Theology focuses on the other rail—it is all about the *Glory of God*. But that is not correct! Dog Theology does not focus entirely on the *Glory of God*. This would be just as incorrect and detrimental as Cat Theology. Remember, Cat Theology is not incorrect, so to leave it out would be just as wrong as when Cat Theology leaves out the glory of God. If our theology runs on a single rail, our "train of faith" will not arrive at its destination. Proper Dog Theology lived out is a balance on both rails with appropriate priorities for each.

- Does God love us? Absolutely, and to leave that out is inappropriate.
- Did Christ die for us? Absolutely, and to leave that out is inappropriate.
- Does God want to bless us? Absolutely, and to leave that out is inappropriate.
- Dog theology involves both messages—God loves us and wants us to point to His glory.

In fact, that is why He died for us—to save us because He loved us and so that we might seek to fulfill our greatest purpose: to live for and pointing to His glory. And that, in turn, is so that we might receive our greatest joy!

There is mutual satisfaction in this process. He wants you to have the best—Him. So, He demands that we point to, exalt, lift-up, and glorify Him because He both deserves it, and it is through this that we receive our greatest joy. Remember the quote from John Piper, "Man is most satisfied when God is most glorified."

Our churches need to be filled with balance. Yes, God loves you and wants to bless you—this is the message that attracts both unbelievers and Cat Christians. That message ought to be there; it is not incorrect. Cats, Dogs, and unbelievers are all attracted to Cat food! But, God also wants us to think in terms of priorities and results. *Why* does He save us? So we may glorify Him for His mercy. *Why* does He bless us? Because it is an outworking of His glory. *Why* does He take us to heaven? So He can show off His glory for ever and ever. *Why* does He command us to live for His glory? Because we ought to and need to in order that we may receive our greatest joy.

We think it is a matter of focus and priority at this point; Cats focus and live primarily giving their attention to receiving the bless-ings—living for the 70 or so years this life offers. Dogs enjoy the attention God gives them in this life, but they focus on the life to come. Cats live for *now*—Dogs live with *eternity* in mind.

What does a Dog church look like? It invites the masses to worship God, both for who He is and what He's done. It invites the lame, the blind, the troubled, those full of misery, and those with lives full of nothing to come and taste of the "living water." Having been refreshed and given life, they are then taught what that life is for and how to live it to the fullest with a focus on God's glory.

If this book has left you with the impression that you need to run back to your church and change everything, you may have misread it—and we may have failed you by giving that impres-sion. (That is why we are including this epilogue.) You do not have to change everything—you just need to devise a way, a plan, a strategy to take the Cats you are attracting and turn them into Dogs. Cat Theology is not wrong—it is only wrong to stay on it and to focus primarily on it at the expense of living for and pointing to God's glory.

Scripture tells us that we are to be changed and transformed by the renewing of our minds. Bring the Cats into the church and then devise a program that is built for the renewing of their minds. This is the educational arm of the church. If you are a Minister of Education, your job is critical at this point. Our vision and plan needs to be enlarged to include as its ultimate goal training Christians for ultimate joy—to glorify God and enjoy Him forever.

If you, like me (Gerald) look back and wondered if you wasted the first years of your ministry by preaching a Cat Theology, then you need to realize this is not entirely correct. These years were not *wasted*—because Cat Theology is not incorrect—but the coming years can be used to bring balance and to adjust the message that this life's ultimate purpose is both to enjoy Him and glorify Him forever.

What is our goal for you? To glorify God by enjoying Him and the blessings He gives you and to play your role in somehow taking this glory to the nations! This way you will live out a life of proper balance and priorities.

For His UnveilinGLORY,
Bob Sjogren and Gerald Robison

A Dog's Glossary of Terms

Because Dogs see life in terms of God's glory, they redefine everything in terms of this. Here are some definitions to help you see how all things are "from him and through him and to him" (Romans 11:36).

Angels: Beings who perfectly obey and reflect His glory.

Church (the): People through whom God wants to display His Glory.

Crisis: An opportunity to show God more glory.

Crucifixion: Jesus' (and the Father's) commitment to upholding the worth of His glory.

Demons: Once-angelic beings who chose to reject God's glory and follow Satan's empty glory.

Depression: An emotional or psychological reaction to not trusting in the glory of God.

Faith: Trusting in the glory of God.

Grace: God giving us His glory when we don't deserve it.

Hell: An everlasting punishment for desecrating and rejecting an infinite glory.

Impatience: Not resting in God's glorious timing.

Justification: God seeing His glory in our lives.

Lust/Greed: Choosing someone or something to be more precious than God's glory.

Marriage: A commitment to reflect the glory of God to, with, and within one special person (of the opposite sex) and to illustrate the relationship of Jesus to the Church.

Parenting: Reflecting the glory of God to the children in your care and training them in the ways of His glory.

Prayer: Calling on God to reveal His glory.

Pride: Taking God's glory for yourself.

Salvation: Falling in love with God's glory.

Sanctification: God's glory being worked into our lives.

Satan: A being who chose to reject God's glory and seek His own and who therefore contrasts with the glory of God.

School: An opportunity to grow in knowledge to better express God's glory.

Sin: Any action or thought that challenges the worth of God's glory.

Spiritual Gifts: Special opportunities to reveal the glory of God through unique talents God has chosen to give you.

Suffering (for God): A magnification of the worth of the glory of the Father.

Work: An opportunity to bring God glory through the gifts and talents He has given you.

Worship: Radiating God's glory back to Him.

Notes

[1] DeVern Fromke, *Unto Full Stature* (Cloverdale, Ind.: Sure Foundation, 2001), p. 17.

[2] James Mulholland, *Praying Like Jesus, The Lord's Prayer in a Culture of Prosperity* (San Francisco: HarperSanFrancisco, 2001), pp. 19–20.

[3] Bob Sjogren, *Unveiled At Last* (Seattle: Crown Ministries International, 1996).

[4] Bruce Wilkinson, *The Prayer of Jabez* (Sisters: Multnomah, 2000).

[5] Donald Grey Barnhouse, *The Invisible War* (Grand Rapids: Zondervan, 1980), p. 31.

[6] Tommy Tenney, *The God Chasers* (Shippensburg, Penn.: Destiny Image, 1999), p. 121.

[7] W.B. Forbush, ed., *Foxe's Book of Martyrs* (Grand Rapids: Zondervan, 1978), p. 12.

[8] Ibid. p. 16.

[9] Ibid. p. 19.

[10] Ibid. p. 22.

[11] Ibid. p. 29.

[12] John F. Walvoord and Roy B. Zuck, *The Bible Knowledge Commentary: An Exposition of the Scriptures by Dallas Seminary Faculty* (Wheaton, Ill.: Victor Books, 1989), p. 307.

[13] William Branham, "The Lamb's Broken Leg," from *Beginning and Ending of the Gentile Dispensation*, sermon given at the Branham Tabernacle (Jeffersonville, Ind.: Jan. 9, 1995). Transcribed from cassette #55-0109E.

[14] John Piper, *Let the Nations be Glad* (Grand Rapids: Baker Book House, 2003).

[15] R. C. Sproul, *The Invisible Hand* (Phillipsburg: P & R Press, 2003).

[16] Larry Crabb, *Shattered Dreams* (Colorado Springs: Waterbrook Press, 2002).

[17] John Piper, *Desiring God* (Sisters: Multnomah, 2003).

[18] *QuickVerse 6 Greek Edition* by Parson's Technology, CD-ROM.

[19] John Piper, *A Hunger for God* (Wheaton: Crossway Books, 1997).

[20] Wayne Rice, *Still More Hot Illustrations for Youth Talks* (El Cajon, Calif.: Youth Specialties, Inc., 1999).

[21] Corrie ten Boom with John Scherrill, *The Hiding Place* (New York: Bantam, 1984).

[22] John Piper, *Let the Nations Be Glad! The Supremacy of God in Missions* (Grand Rapids: Baker Book House, 1993), p. 1.

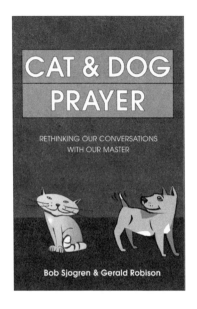

When we first become believers, our natural tendency is still to be self-absorbed, especially in how we pray. As a result, our prayers are more of a laundry list that revolves around "me" and my needs and comfort.

Because God rarely answers these kinds of prayer, many of us quickly give up on praying, believing that God doesn't answer prayer. As a result, we end up checking in from time to time making sure he knows we're there and reminding him of our needs—hoping he'll do something about them.

Cat and Dog Prayer will help move you from self-centered prayers to God-focused prayers. You'll learn how to pray, as the authors show:

- How to pray prayers that God wants to answer,
- How you've been given a "Blank Check" by God,
- The six reasons why God says "Wait,"
- The four reasons why God says "No,"
- How to pray "Cause Me Prayers" releasing the Holy Spirit completely in your life, and
- How you need to be careful about what you pray about—because it can be the very thing that takes you away from God himself!

This book will change the way you pray. It is a natural outflow of *Cat and Dog Theology*.

Paperback, 121 pages, 5.5 x 8.5
ISBN: 978-1-60657-043-2
Retail: $13.99

Available for purchase online or through your local bookstore.

ALSO AVAILABLE

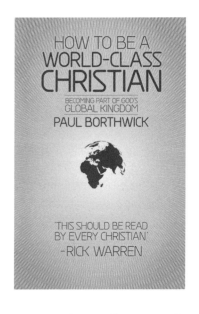

"There is a YOU-shaped hole in God's Kingdom—find it and fill it."
—Patrick Johnstone

How to Be a World-Class Christian reveals God's unfolding drama throughout the world and how you can become part of that story. It will show you how to expand your understanding of God's heart for the nations as it is revealed throughout Scripture. It will increase your global prayer life and align your passions with God's. Using practical tools and observations from everyday life, this book invites each one of us to stretch our knowledge of the purposes of God right at home and throughout the world and then to take the steps necessary to start responding to the opportunities we face. Finding and filling the place in the world that God has designed for you is what *How to Be a World-Class Christian* is designed to do.

In *Purpose-Driven Life*, Rick Warren cites Paul Borthwick's books *A Mind For Missions* and *How to Be a World-Class Christian* as resources that "should be read by every Christian."

Paperback, 237 pages, 5.5 x 8.5
ISBN: 978-1-93406-834-2
Retail: $14.99

Available for purchase online or through your local bookstore.

ALSO AVAILABLE

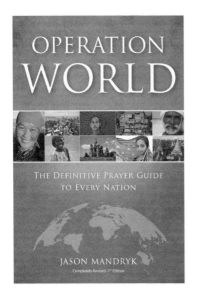

Join millions of praying people around the world using this book to inform, inspire, and ignite their prayers. Engage your heart and mind in global prayer with this thoroughly researched, fully-updated seventh edition. It is loaded with clear, concise, accurate information on peoples, languages, religions, denominations, spiritual trends, and prayer needs—for every country in the world, from the largest to the smallest.

Operation World's easy-to-follow summaries of every nation include:

- Timely challenges for prayer and specific answers to prayer
- Updates on church growth, with a focus on evangelicals
- Population, people group and language statistics
- Charts and maps showing global religious and demographic trends
- Explanations of major currents in economics, politics and society

Leading evangelical mission leaders, scholars, writers, pastors and lay people all over the world rely on this book, refer to it, and quote from it regularly. Every fact, number and statement is checked and re-checked with global and local experts in each field.

1012 pages, 6 x 9
Paperback ISBN: 978-1-85078-862-1, Retail: $17.99
Paperback/CD Combo ISBN: 978-1-85078-875-1, Retail: $39.99
Hardback ISBN: 978-1-85078-861-4, Retail: $34.99

Available for purchase online or through your local bookstore.

COMING SOON

THE OTHER SIDE OF THE CROSS

BOB SJOGREN AND KEVIN KIMBROUGH

Bob Sjogren and Kevin Kimbrough have teamed up to unmask conflicting and confusing teaching present throughout the church. What is this cancerous teaching? At times we are told, "It's all about God." Yet at other times we are told, "It's all about us!" Which is it?

Most of us don't realize that there are two sides to the cross and we are familiar with only one side: Jesus died for our sin. But there is another side. Jesus died for the glory of the Father. By fixing our eyes on the familiar side of the cross, we develop a "Meology" bent on one primary purpose: keeping the rules of our faith for the sake of being blessed by God. Understanding the other side of the cross yields an aspiration to a higher calling in life: living to make God famous no matter what the cost!

A significant question faces the church today: Are these two sides of the cross equal, or is one side greater than the other? Answering that question will resolve the conflicting and confusing teaching and force us to take a deep look into the glory of God. For it is God's glory (not God's blessings) that should be the central theme of our lives.

Discover a theology worth living for. Discover a theology worth dying for. Discover the other side of the cross!

Paperback, 224 pages, 5.5 x 8.5
ISBN: 978-1-60657-086-9
Retail: $15.99

Available September 2011.